Dressing for England

SUNY series, Studies in the Long Nineteenth Century

Pamela K. Gilbert, editor

Dressing for England

Fashion and Nationalism in Victorian Novels

AMY L. MONTZ

SUNY
PRESS

Cover credit: Brooklyn Museum Costume Collection at The Metropolitan Museum of Art, Gift of the Brooklyn Museum, 2009; Gift of Alice Welles, 1933. Public domain.

Published by State University of New York Press, Albany

EU GPSR Authorised Representative:
Logos Europe, 9 rue Nicolas Poussin, 17000, La Rochelle, France
contact@logoseurope.eu

For information, contact State University of New York Press, Albany, NY
www.sunypress.edu

Library of Congress Cataloging-in-Publication Data

Name: Montz, Amy L., author.
Title: Dressing for England : fashion and nationalism in Victorian novels / Amy L. Montz.
Description: Albany : State University of New York Press, [2025]. | Series: SUNY series, studies in the long nineteenth century | Includes bibliographical references and index.
Identifiers: LCCN 2025017370 | ISBN 9798855804782 (hardcover : alk. paper) | ISBN 9798855804805 (ebook) | ISBN 9798855804799 (pbk. : alk. paper)
Subjects: LCSH: English fiction—19th century—History and criticism. | Fashion in literature. | Nationalism in literature. | Literature and society—England—History—19th century. | LCGFT: Literary criticism.
Classification: LCC PR878.F34 M66 2025 | DDC 823/.809357—dc23/eng/20250615
LC record available at https://lccn.loc.gov/202501737

*For Anthony, who, as my shining light, never diminishes,
never wavers, always supplies warmth and comfort.*

Moreover, isn't written Fashion a literature?

— Roland Barthes, *The Fashion System*

Contents

List of Illustrations   ix

Acknowledgments   xi

Introduction   Ladies' Business, Feminine Weakness, Fashionable Dress   1

Chapter One   "That Wicked Paris": Elizabeth Gaskell Fashions the Good Englishwoman   23

Chapter Two   William Thackeray's Fashionable Humbugs and Unfashionable Darlings: Consuming National Distinctions of Dress   47

Chapter Three   "The Will and Pleasure of Women": The Feminine Love of Fashion in George Eliot's *Middlemarch*   65

Chapter Four   "Now She's All Hat and Ideas": Fashioning the British Suffrage Movement   83

Conclusion   To Have and to Wear: National Distinctions of Dress in Royal Weddings   105

Notes   117

Works Cited   137

Index   147

Illustrations

Figure 1.1   Thomson's Empress Crinoline in Red   23

Figure 2.1   Roxey Ann Caplin's Corset 1851   47

Figure 3.1   Photograph of George Eliot   67

Figure 3.2   More Detailed Photograph of George Eliot   68

Figure 4.1   Black Silk Stockings Worn by the Suffragette
             Lillian Burslem   83

Figure 4.2   Imperial Pageant, Women's Coronation Procession   90

Figure 4.3   Group of Suffragettes in the Costume of England,
             Scotland, Ireland, and Wales   92

Figure 4.4   A Lancashire Lass in Clogs and Shawl   97

Acknowledgments

Dressing for England is, as one of my students told me, old enough to go to college, and she is right. I have been working on this book in one form or another—preliminary exams, dissertation, articles, and now full-length book—since 2006, and I have relied heavily on so many people for funding, for archival research, and for support that I hardly know where to begin.

First, I'd like to thank the University of New Hampshire Press for permission to reprint my *Vanity Fair* chapter from *Crossings in Text and Textile* edited by Katherine Joslin and Daneen Wardrop in 2015. Also, a version of my suffragette chapter was published in *Critical Studies in Fashion and Beauty* in 2012.

Funding: I am grateful to both Texas A&M University, College Station, and the University of Southern Indiana for a myriad of funding opportunities both in graduate school and in my professional career. At A&M, I want to thank the Department of English and its Graduate Studies Program, Dr. James Rosenheim and the Melbern G. Glasscock Center for Humanities Research, the Women's Studies Program, and the Senator Phil Gramm Doctoral Fellowship Award, all of which awarded me substantial funding to travel to archives for research abroad or allowed me time during the semester off of teaching to work on my project.

At the University of Southern Indiana, I am grateful to the Department of English and chair Oana Popescu-Sandu, the College of Liberal Arts and Deans Del Doughty, Kristalyn Shefveland, and Silvia Rode for funding for the indexing and imaging. I also want to thank the College of Liberal Arts and the Office of Sponsored Projects and Research for funding multiple archival trips to England and Scotland. I am also grateful to the Provost's Office and the Board of Trustees for awarding me a sabbatical in spring 2020 to work on this book. This project could not have been possible without the generous support I received during my time as a graduate student and my time as a professor.

Archival research: There have been many, many archives that have contributed their collections to the research for this book. I am most grateful to Beverley Cook at the London Museum for her infinite help in the suffrage archives, to Beatrice Behlen at the London Museum for help in the fashion archives, and to Richard Dabb for his help with imaging. At the Fashion Museum in Bath, I am most grateful for the staff and collections manager Fleur Johnson for several trips to the archives and one harrowing one right before the COVID-19 lockdown. The Victoria and Albert Museum archives are a wealth of treasures, as is the Women's Library at the London School of Economics and Political Science. I would like to thank the museum in Paisley, Scotland, for allowing me to look at pattern books and older machines, which in turn helped me understand the labor behind the making of Paisley shawls. Of course, I must thank the British Library for its excellent preservation of fashionable tracts, such as the one that insists women were killing children with their crinolines. Other archives and collections, too, were visited but their collections do not appear in this text, and I am grateful for the help of a dozen archives, archivists, and collection managers.

I want to thank the interlibrary loan staff at both Texas A&M and the University of Southern Indiana (USI), especially Kirsten Williams. I literally would not have been able to get any of my work done without their tireless efforts and ability to find rare materials. Thank you for your hard work and for enjoying my fashion searches! I also want to thank Jillian Jones in the Dean's Office at USI, and Caitlin Woolsey in the English Office at USI, for help with imaging, scanning, and other support.

Support: Dr. Mary Ann O'Farrell directed my dissertation and influenced my work greatly, but most importantly, she helped nurture my work on fashion and nationalism in Victorian novels from a germ of an idea in a seminar class as the result of reading Gaskell's *Cranford*, Thackeray's *Vanity Fair*, and Sarah Stickney Ellis's *The Women of England* together. Somewhere in my files is still the email I sent to her when the idea for my dissertation began to take place. My other dissertation committee members, Dr. Melanie Hawthorne, Dr. Lynne Vallone, and Dr. Sally Robinson, were supportive throughout my process and into my job search afterward. I am most grateful to my committee for their help, their support, and their belief in this project.

Dr. Stephen Spencer, Dr. Julia Galbus-Kiesel, and Dr. Oana Popescu-Sandu have been my department chairs over my time at USI and have supported this project through recommendation letters, course release support, and general cheerleading. Deans Michael Aakhus, James Beeby, Melinda Roberts, and Del Doughty have also supported this project through approvals for course releases and funding opportunities.

I would be remiss if I did not thank my faithful writing partner, Dr. Dana E. Lawrence, whose dedication to our thrice-a-week writing schedule was instrumental in beginning and finishing this project as a book rather than a dissertation. Other friends have also been supportive, including Dr. Andrea Adolph, Dr. Abby Bowers, Dr. Maggie Morris Davis, Dr. Sara K. Day, Dr. Sonya Sawyer Fritz, Dr. Meghan Gilbert, Dr. Kristalyn Shefveland, Dr. Laura Soderberg, Dr. Melissa Stacer, and Dr. Gina Terry, all of whom read drafts and cheered me on along the process.

I am most grateful for my anonymous reviewers at SUNY Press, whose infinitely helpful, honest, and supportive feedback was most appreciated. Rebecca Colesworthy is a wonderful editor and very generous with her time and emails, and, along with Dr. Pamela K. Gilbert, series editor, saw the possibility of this text and helped bring it into the world.

Finally, none of this would have been possible without the love and support of my family: my husband, Anthony Rintala, and my father, Byron Montz. Anthony read drafts upon drafts of these chapters, answered odd questions in the early morning hours ("Which do you like better: the crinoline or the corset?"), and managed the household and the dogs while I galivanted off to England and Scotland for research. My father, whose support has always existed, often jokes that he wanted me to know how to read well as a child, but he didn't know I'd take it *this* far. I love you both, and I thank the world every day I have you two and my pups in my life.

Introduction

Ladies' Business, Feminine Weakness, Fashionable Dress

The love of dress is a growing evil, capable of any extravagance, or of any folly to gratify its depraved taste; it is not the love of beauty, or of outward elegance and refinement; for every day we see beauty outraged, and nature deformed, by the tortuous inventions of fashion for their adornment. It is a *mania*, a *passion*, a delusion that spreads its baneful influence through every grade of society: a yawning gulf into which, like the one of old, the wealth of a nation is unavailingly cast. (6–7)

—Anonymous, *Dress, A Few Words on*
Fashion and Her Idols (1859)

No other ladies, except the English, thus transgress all the rules of toilette. They alone look awkward and badly-dressed everywhere except at home; and I take the liberty of calling their attention to the fact. (157)

—Chroniqueuse, *Photographs of Paris Life:*
A Record of the Politics, Art, Fashion,
and Anecdote of Paris During the Past Eighteen Months (1861)

"I have never undervalued dress," [Phoebe] said, "as some girls do; I think it is a very important social influence." (120)

—Margaret Oliphant, *Phoebe Junior,*
A Last Chronicle of Carlingford (1876)

When we think about it closely, what does the word "dressing" mean, exactly? One meaning is to put on clothes, to clothe oneself, which may be the most common definition of the word. Or perhaps the most common definition would be to put on top of, like dressing a table. Those both are verbs. What of nouns? Dressing is a word for the objects on top of other objects, like clothes on bodies, or creamy ranch on lettuce. Perhaps I digress with salad, but it, too, comes to mind.

Let us think also of dressing *for* something, like an event. That becomes an action, a verb with import. To dress *for* an event is to physically put on clothes but also to carefully choose appropriate clothing for said event. A wedding, for example, is an entirely different act of "dressing *for*" than a run to Target, or, at least, it should be. But to think about dressing *for*, say, England, as is the title of this work, we are back into noun and verb dichotomy. Is it an action, or is it a textile? I mean it to be both because, as I argue in this work, women dressed *for* England by declaring their nationalism through their clothing and their textiles, but also, women were *dressing* for England, in that they decorated the nation and became representative of its place in the global landscape. A noun and a verb, both together, at the same time, pinioned by a preposition and held together by the bodies that are the very dressing we discuss.

In reviewing nineteenth-century texts about fashion, we would find an overwhelming proliferation of judgments on the importance of dress to a nation: its role in social influence, as Phoebe tells us in the third epigraph that begins this introduction; its usefulness in distinguishing national citizens, as Chroniqueuse describes in the second epigraph; and its dangerousness to a nation at large, as the anonymous author of *Dress* warns in the first. For many writers in the nineteenth century, fashionable dress could inform, delight, disgust, and influence. It could also cause panic and obsession; promote political causes; designate class status or national origin; determine a woman's character, wealth, or intention; or be an object of beauty to attract the eye. All three texts that begin this chapter insist that dress can be an empowering arena through which women gain some semblance of command over their selves; even in the passage from *Dress,* which views such an arena negatively, dress is an incredibly powerful tool in both the symbolic and literal "separate spheres" in which many critics believe Victorian women existed.[1] But all three texts react to this empowering arena differently. Both public and private, both personal and social, dress is neither solely in the domestic home nor solely in the city streets. Dress is private; it covers the naked body and is worn next to the skin. Dress is personal; it is chosen by the wearer according to taste and current fashion trends. Dress is public; it completes the self and is an outward display of will. Dress is social; it is a common uniting factor among all people, as all people cover and protect the body in some way. To be undressed is, as Anne Hollander argues in *Seeing Through Clothes*, a less "natural" state than to be dressed; the body is clothed more hours of the day than it is unclothed.[2] In this sense, then, dress is both natural and artificial, and this ill-defined, nebulous state of dress allows it to be scripted and interpreted in order to convey meaning. Therefore, even when it is "just a dress"—a gendered article of clothing to cover the body—it is never "just a dress"—a trivial garment worn by trivial female members of society. Dress does real work in social circles, because it can be used to convey meaning such as class status, recognizable standards of fashion, or, in this book's main argument, national allegiance, affiliation, or abhorrence. In accepting that a dress is never "just a dress," we understand that clothing can speak with or without its wearer's intent and convey meaning to the viewer, to the wearer, or to society at large.

Further, by capturing fashion through photography and by recording the minute details of dress in both fictional and nonfictional texts, the nineteenth century insisted that dress was important enough to record. The Victorian era, marked by vast technological innovation, saw an explosion of cheaper printing and thus the insertion of more fashion magazines into its burgeoning media market.[3] Further, these innovations led to the proliferation of ready-made clothing available for indiscriminate purchasing through innovations in manufacture and, of course, photography that captured the fashions and dress of persons from every class. Because of its intimate connection with the body—dress covers the naked flesh—dress was oftentimes discussed as the public revelation of the private self. But because dress is in constant flux due to shifting fashion trends, personal choice, and whimsy, dress could suggest artificiality, inconsistency, and manipulation. Margaret Oliphant's character Phoebe understands this: dress is not to be undervalued for its usefulness in influencing society. By announcing that dress is "an important social influence," Phoebe argues for the use of dress as the manipulation of feminine presentation; she can construct a self that may or may not be her authentic self. The anonymous author of *Dress* thus argues that dress is not to be trusted for its "baneful influence" irreparably damaging to the "wealth of the nation," so when Chroniqueuse claims to be able to distinguish Englishwomen from Frenchwomen strictly by examining their clothing, she reiterates an insistence on national distinctions of dress and style evident through the bodies of women. But by using the word "transgress," Chroniqueuse suggests that the Englishwomen are conscious of their unfashionability, and thus she puts forth an argument for the construction of style. This construction—the artificiality of clothing that is not to be undervalued—and its influence over nation offer a form of feminine power in a century and a country defined by the dichotomy between its ideological passivity of middle-class women and the female monarch on its throne.

All three passages help elucidate this book's argument that at the same time nineteenth-century England viewed dress and particularly fashionable dress as a trivial feminine weakness, it also viewed it as a dangerous tool with which women maintained, manipulated, and controlled the way that they were perceived. Nineteenth-century women used fashion and dress, heretofore dismissed socially and nationally as an inconsequential feminine concern, to express Englishness abroad, or to influence society at home, or just to convey extravagance, beauty, or elegance, as these introductory texts suggest. By doing so, these women turned the world of fashion and dress into an arena of feminine power in which they could make choices and decisions that could and would impact themselves, their families, their society, and, in this book's ultimate argument, their nation. When women used fashion as a tool with which they communicated personal and national affiliations and constructed selves through artificial means, they challenged the commonly held beliefs in the insignificance of fashion and dress. I argue that fashion and dress did real work in Victorian England and do real work in its literature. This book examines the simultaneous celebration over, anxiety of, and concern for women's fashion and dress reiterated through the era's texts. With that examination, I argue for Victorian England's understanding of women's fashion and dress as significant rather than trivial, dangerous rather than frivolous, tools as well as threats to the established paradigm of Victorian English womanhood. Victorian women, through their use of contemporary understandings of the nationality of dress, displayed allegiance to or disillusionment with nation, and the century's novels, textiles, and ephemera reveal a nation's social concerns, political crises, and the fabric of its everyday domesticity.

Fashion and Nationalism in Context

I do not claim to be the first literary critic to detail the anatomy of nineteenth-century women's clothing or the first to discuss the importance of fashion and dress to literature, to history, or to culture. Katherine Joslin's exquisitely detailed discussion of a dress in *Edith Wharton and the Making of Fashion*, for example, reminds us that dresses had two audiences: public and private. The inside of a dress was a private space meant to be seen by wearer and creator (and perhaps lady's maid) alone, while the outside of a dress, upon a very close look, reveals intimate details and intricate trimmings that display signs of wealth and status to an audience eager and willing to decipher them (53–57). Daneen Wardrop's *Emily Dickinson and the Labor of Clothing* reads the author's work with her physical textiles and photographic image as evidence, while Clair Hughes's *Dressed in Fiction* explores clothing in great detail through the literature in which it was displayed. As Joslin notes, "It is a strange experience for a literary scholar, schooled in the subtleties of language, to research actual garments and literally to read dress" (53). But it is an important one, as Joslin and other critics like her use the textiles, dresses, and material culture of the nineteenth century to help illuminate its literatures for a twenty-first-century audience. We cannot pretend to understand the importance of textiles, dress, and fashion in nineteenth-century literature if we do not first understand their importance for the audience literate in that dress's meaning, codes, and terminology. This duality of text and textile, of literature and dress, is an important factor in determining social navigation, codes, and contexts and, for the purposes of this book's argument, in understanding how fashion and dress can convey national allegiance or abhorrence to an audience literate in its signs, meanings, and displays.

Due to its cyclical nature, fashion is constantly marked by change, and Elizabeth Wilson argues that "Fashion, in a sense *is* change" (3, emphasis original). For many fashion theorists and historians, fashion is capable of transmitting and communicating information, and perhaps it is even fashion's intention. Fred Davis notes that "any definition of *fashion* seeking to grasp what distinguishes it from style, custom, conventional or acceptable dress, or prevalent modes must place its emphasis on the element of *change* we often associate with the term" and sees that change as "some shift in the relationship of signifier and signified" (14, emphasis original). As fashion is defined by constant change, so is its ability to be defined by constantly shifting meanings. The interpretation of fashion shifts on various levels, including personal, social, and political, but the use of fashion to convey personal or social meanings and intentions is in constant flux as well. Part of the concern the author of *Dress* expresses over the "growing evil" that the love of fashion presents is not necessarily the outrage of beauty, the deformity of nature, or the excessive vanity of women, but rather the fact that fashion is an unstable communicator that can be used to convey and to manipulate socially understood meanings of dress. Most importantly, as characters like Phoebe show us, women understand that clothing can be manipulated; this is problematic for nineteenth-century England because women's manipulation of fashion makes fashion useful and purposeful rather than trivial.

The reason that novels often describe dress when establishing characters seems self-explanatory; there seems to be a commonly held assumption that dress will convey something about its wearer. A description of a character's dress may seem arbitrary or merely part of the novelist's style; William Thackeray, for example, is a great detailer of items of dress in his novels. But in a century marked by rapid technological change, and in a genre that reaches its pinnacle of respect and popularity during this time, many nineteenth-century novels offer details of dress that are purposeful beyond the establishment of character. I argue that fashion does real work in nineteenth-century literature, as details of dress, a woman's love of finery, or even a character's attitude toward clothing—Phoebe's understanding of dress as an important social tool—can convey national meaning as it speaks to an audience that understands that fashion can be read. Diana Crane marks clothing as "one of the most visible forms of consumption" that "performs a major role in the social construction of identity" (1), while fashion is more specifically defined by "strong norms about appropriate appearances at a particular point in time" (1). This "social construction of identity" is for Crane often culturally specific (1) and can be used within the culture to gain position or status (5). Anne Hollander agrees with the idea that clothing can "suggest, persuade, connote, insinuate, or indeed lie, and apply subtle pressure while their wearer is speaking frankly and straightforwardly of other matters" (355), and the "subtle pressure" becomes, when applied to novels, the background description of a character's dress. These details of dress can belie the statements of their wearer, just as the statements of the wearer can belie the details of dress. When those novelistic details of dress reveal national affiliations, prejudices, or meanings, dress can "suggest, persuade, connote, insinuate, or indeed lie" at the same time it can "apply subtle pressure" about national concerns.

Throughout the nineteenth century, England faced numerous social, political, and technological changes that more often than not were influenced by the expansion of the empire. No longer did the designation "Britishness" strictly refer to Wales, Ireland, England, and Scotland. In expanding outward to include countries like India, the British Empire complicated the insular understanding of "British" as defining those peoples who live within close proximity to England.[4] Further, as the expanding Empire acquired more people, England contracted inward in an attempt to establish definitively what it meant to be English and, in particular, what it meant to be an Englishman or Englishwoman. Angelia Poon argues that "The power that comes from being English in the Victorian period is crucially dependent on a categorizing imperative that establishes and structures a series of distinctions such as those between citizen and foreigner, colonizer and colonized, and metropole and colony" (501).[5] But if the empire begins to blur the lines between "citizen and foreigner, colonizer and colonized," then that "categorizing imperative" begins to break down; it then becomes increasingly difficult to distinguish those identifications. This responsibility of identification falls on the English citizen, who must establish both how to recognize Englishness and how to convey Englishness.

To distinguish oneself as English, one must distinguish what it is to be not-English, that is, to be foreign.[6] Expressions of nationalist pride or nationalism, which Peter Alter defines as existing "whenever individuals feel they belong primarily to the nation, and whenever affective attachment and loyalty to that nation override all other attachments and loyalties" (9), establish a commonality between citizens. One is English because one expresses "affective attachment and loyalty" for England; these sentiments are, in Alter's estimation, dependent on a feeling of national belonging. Linda Colley's *Britons: Forging the Nation 1707–1837* sees this distinction between English and not-English as a result of the confrontation with "an obviously alien 'Them'" which leads "an otherwise diverse community [to] become a reassuring or merely desperate 'Us'" (6). In Colley's estimation, this occurs for Britain in the period just prior to Queen Victoria's reign.[7] The Victorian era inherits the larger crisis of national definition seen in the period during and just following the Napoleonic Wars; fears of invasion and the expansion of imperial forces are writ in Victorian novels as fears of social invasion and concerns over the expanding empire.[8]

This constantly shifting definition of Britishness, no longer composed of physical proximity to England, forced England to establish standards not only for nation but also for gender. While it seems self-explanatory that nation constantly influences its citizens' lives, it cannot be said that all the nation's citizens will have an impact on it. The majority of England's male citizens, especially those who fit within the parameters of the white middle-class masculinity prized by Victorian England, had the power to vocalize national concerns through the vote, through public office, or through authoring texts. Its female citizens, however, regardless of class, race, or education, often were relegated to a national impact that was only symbolic in resonance.[9] Joanne Sharp's "Gendering Nationhood: A Feminist Engagement with National Identity" argues that "The female is a prominent *symbol* of nationalism and honour. But this is a symbol to be protected by masculine agency" (100, emphasis original). Without the agency to enact fully the responsibilities of a national citizen, Victorian women were held up as symbols, even national treasures, that the men had to protect and maintain; this symbolism was established through ideology that claimed to define what a "true" Englishwoman was.

The Victorian era established the character of an Englishwoman in no small way through her rejection or obsession with dress. A "true" English-woman rejects fashion and thus rejects the potential manipulative powers of fashion.[10] An overt "love of dress" is, as the author of *Dress* reminds us, disastrous to the wealth of a nation because it represents women's utilization of fashion. Englishness becomes definable not only by action but also by appearance, as *Photographs of Paris Life* argues, and thus Englishness in women becomes increasingly dependent on outward displays of fashion because fashionable dress is so recognizable and easily distinguishable. Further, more subtle descriptions of a character's attitude toward fashionable dress can help distinguish between "Us" and "Them." In order to distinguish between "Us" and "Them," Victorian novelists utilize the "subtle pressure" of dress description that Hollander identifies. Details of dress, particularly fashionable dress, become markers of national distinction. The continuous change that is the very definition of fashion parallels the expansion and contraction of England and the British Empire, and several Victorian novels detail how shifts in fashion and nation often are coupled. The popularity of the Indian shawl or women's turbans, two foreign articles of clothing domesticated in England, reflect the empire's Eastern conquests, while the height of the crinoline and the decline of the corset, both associated with greater freedom of movement for women, represent the beginnings of the women's rights movement. Exploring particular articles of women's clothing like the Indian shawl, the crinoline, or the corset help us understand what is important to Victorian women during a time that often associated them with so-called feminine weaknesses like fashion.

To convince ourselves that fashion is a roving entity that offers women no control over their own bodies, choices, and desires is to convince ourselves that Victorian women had no power at all, socially, politically, or personally. But there is agency in choice, even when working within the fashion system itself. This understanding of choice, the modicum of power and agency within a larger system, is symbolic of those middle-class women's struggle to find similar power and agency within the larger system of nation. Nineteenth-century Englishwomen did have power in limited arenas and classes; it is important that we never discount this power and women's ability to work within these systems to articulate their understanding of nation, politics, and society, as well as their ability to gain more power within the system. Here, ultimately, is where the crux of this book's argument lies: fashion, as I argue, is not a weakness at all but rather a tool of extraordinary personal, social, and national power for women during a time that would deny them the majority access to all three arenas. Further, I argue that not only did Victorian women passively receive a national distinction of Englishness through their fashion and dress; they purposefully and decisively constructed an English or non-English self in order to convey their social, personal, or national power. Men's clothing too speaks and conveys these forms of power. It can be national and fashionable, and it can be important and essential. But nineteenth-century England did not afford women the same rights, respect, or position within the establishment of the nation as it afforded its men. Women often were symbolic representations of nation; they could symbolize the importance of nation for the nation itself or could be representative of the larger concerns of the nation, but regardless of class or wealth, they were denied more substantial or concrete forms of power, most notably, the vote. I explore the understanding of fashion and nationalism in Victorian novels specifically through the presentation of women's clothing because, as I argue, women's dress, that feminine realm to which Victorian England dismissed its women, offers women an instrument with which to articulate the national and personal concerns their nation would not grant them. Victorian women thus break free from the association with national symbolism to instead employ agency in their enactment of national representation.

Nationalism and "Good English Strawberries"

In such a time of globalization we may find it difficult to imagine nationalism being so important to contemporary persons. Certainly, we see calls to "shop local" or "buy American," but as so many of our products are foreign made (even the items declaring "buy American" often have a "made in China" label, like the MAGA hats of the 2016 presidential election), it seems like people might not even care that products are not English, or American. But an encounter I overheard in the railway station on my way to Paisley, Scotland, to study the shawls created there in the town in imitation of the expensive Kashmir shawls proved to me that nationalism is as important now as it was in the nineteenth century. In Marks and Spencer, as I was purchasing snacks, I overheard a woman ask her companion, "Why don't they sell good English strawberries? They're in season" as she looked at the foreign fruits for purchase before her. This instance was of course before Brexit was even on anyone's minds, but in 2011, 150 years after these shawls in Paisley were thought of or produced, Englishwomen still are looking to buy domestic items. The designation was important to me: *good English strawberries*. Were they good because they were English? That seemed to be what the woman was implying. English strawberries, she seemed to say, are superior to other strawberries. And while Kashmir shawls were thought to be superior to domestic shawls—in cost, in manufacture, in production—Paisley shawls allowed the egalitarian presentation of women because they were affordable and recognizable. The domestic item became the democratic item and, thus, the nationalistic item. As fashion and manners tracts urged women to shop domestic, in the same way we see now the call to "Shop local" or "Shop small," to support small local businesses, shopping domestic was the *morally right* thing to do.[11]

So how did fashion and nationalism become so intertwined in the nineteenth century in England? Surprising no one, I am sure, is the revelation that this was not unique to the nineteenth century, to England, or to fashion and textiles. Roze Hentschell has argued for the connection between nationalism and fashion in the seventeenth century, noting that "While clothing may have confirmed national origin in its unworn state, the donning of apparel by actual bodies often disrupted this imaginary national clarity. Wearing foreign clothes disrupted the way of knowing one's country of origin and, perhaps more upsetting, where one's loyalty lay" (544). Hentschell's work is essential in understanding cloth in the seventeenth century, and her focus on the poetry and tracts of the time is a fascinating read. We differ in our discussion not only through time period but also through the focus on gender; I argue for women's clothing's connection to nationalism because women were denied a voice in nationalism, despite the presence and reign of Queen Victoria. William Keenan notes that "Dress is clearly neither culturally nor politically neutral. It is loaded with significance" (181). This significance is, as I argue, often read in the nineteenth century as morally or politically charged. Elaine Chalus looks at the women of the eighteenth century and argues that they, too, used fashion to express political (rather than national) allegiance. She notes, "By turning their dress and accessories to advantage, women could make discreet or obvious political statements. They became participants in, as opposed to spectators of, political life, and contributed to the creation of a larger public sphere" (93).

In Ellen Wood's 1861 novel *East Lynne,* for example, two candidates are opposed in running for member of Parliament (MP) and "all people were eager to testify their respect for Mr. Carlyle. Miss Carlyle was in a great grandeur; a brocaded dress, and a scarlet-and-purple bow in front of it, the size of the pumpkin. It was about the only occasion, in all Miss Carlyle's life, that she had considered it necessary to attire herself magnificently. Barbara wore no bow, but she exhibited a splendid bouquet of scarlet-and-purple flowers. Mr. Carlyle had himself given it to her that morning" (588). The rest of the women, to display their "vote" for Mr. Carlyle, in response to the declaration "Carlyle and honour forever" (588) "shook their handkerchiefs, and displayed their scarlet-and-purple colours" (588).[12] The display of patriotism and, in this book's argument, nationalism, comes as a surprise to some because, as Tamar Meyer reminds us, nations have "largely been constructed as hetero-male project[s]" (6), which leaves women not as producers of nation, but rather symbols of the nation itself, "feminized and characterized as in need of protection; women are figured as the biological and cultural reproducers of the nation" (10). In this sense then, it seems only logical that fashion would be an arena in which women could culturally reproduce the nation.

The symbolic use of fashion and nationalism in England runs into a slight snag, however, because of course, so much of fashion originates in France. David Gilbert argues that "the cachet of the name 'Paris' depends not just on the sustained intensity of the virtual city of promotion campaigns and the fashion press, but also on the credibility of the city as a centre of fashion consumption and particularly as an embodied experience of fashion" (9) but does not discount London as the same: "If in the late eighteenth century London's position as a commercial city created new forms of the fashion process, by the mid-nineteenth century London's imperial centrality was the most significant influence on its development as one of fashion's world capitals. During the nineteenth century, London came to be understood as a site both of innovation and of fashion authority, in the British empire and beyond" (16). However, in "Reflections on Victorian Fashion Plates," Sharon Marcus has argued, "Despite historiographical claims about the role dress played in creating national identity, British fashion after the Napoleonic wars was transatlantic, and British fashion illustration *was* French. Most French fashion magazines published international coeditions, and the major British fashion magazines had Parisian offices and employed French artists to illustrate Parisian trends" (11). Diana Crane in *Fashion and Its Social Agendas: Class, Gender, and Identity in Clothing* has also argued for fashion's origins in France in the nineteenth century, noting that "Because clothing styles for women originated in France, they were heavily coded with a particular set of values about the role of women, specifically the ideal role of the French bourgeois matron" (29). And while I agree that many fashions *originate* in France, I do not agree that it means England did not have a fashion of its own. C. Willett Cunnington in his exhaustive study *English Women's Clothing in the Nineteenth Century* (1937) discusses the differences between French fashion plates and English ones and states, "And always we have to discriminate between fashions purely French and those which were accepted in this country" (6). England responded to what it deemed outrageous French fashions and in turn changed them to make them suitable for England and Englishwomen. By changing the origins of fashion to suit a different taste, and by using and promoting fabrics that were English-made, Englishwomen, English magazines, and English dressmakers were participating in a global fashion system that still exists today.

Therefore, ultimately, fashion speaks. It conveys a language that communicates a variety of messages to a literate audience. Roland Barthes in *The Fashion System* (1983) notes the similarities between written fashion and literature and states, "Fashion and literature in fact utilize a common technique whose end is seemingly to transform an object into language: it is *description*" (12). Further, he argues that "Fashion becomes an autonomous cultural object, with its own original structure and, probably, with a new finality . . . through the language which henceforth takes charge of it. Fashion becomes *narrative*" (277). Jennie Batchelor argues that "Dress—as a signifier of gender, status, and sexuality—is a site around which multiple and competing anxieties are simultaneously focused" (115). Fred Davis in *Fashion, Culture, and Identity* begins by asking, "Is clothing not virtually a visual *language*, with its own distinctive grammar, syntax, and vocabulary?" (3).

But even more so, fashion conveys wealth, class, privilege, morality, personal choice, the viewer's preference, and the wearer's preference, that is to say, it conveys a multitude of messages both conscious and unconscious that was read. Christine Bayles Kortsch argues in *Dress Culture in Late Victorian Women's Fiction: Literacy, Textiles, and Activism* that "Victorian women's dual literacy [in texts as well as textiles] created modes of communication that linked them to other women in what Benedict Anderson, in the context of a discussion of nationalism, calls an 'imagined community'" (10). I see this "imagined community" both belonging to women and fashion as well as women and nation.[13] Women could read outward signs of fashion for signs of inner beliefs. For the Victorian audience, for example, looseness implied loose morals, which in turn implied Frenchness. Therefore, women wore corsets. To be seen without a corset was to be "loose," immoral, and as those terms were associated with foreignness, with Frenchwomen. A good Englishwoman, therefore, was a woman who was laced into her corset so that her figure was compressed.[14]

Who decides what clothing communicates is a more difficult question to answer, because while of course we want to say "society," we have to think of what "society" defines. Entwistle in *The Fashioned Body* argues that "the body is the means by which an individual comes to know and live in a culture" (14). For the Victorians, it was increasingly the middle class that defined the society with sway over fashion, social mores, politics, and not the aristocracy as we saw in eras previous. The middle and working classes were fashion-forward, power-driven classes with power in the nineteenth century and, still, in the twenty-first century. This distinction is a belief solely in the trickle-down theory of fashion[15] when, in fact, more recently, fashion theorists have argued for a trickle-up theory.[16] Street wear, for example, continues to be a major part of fashion labels, who look to the young, the hip, the urban for inspiration. These designers literally look to the urban youth in the larger cities of America and Europe for what true fashion calls for.

Dani Cavallaro and Alexandra Warwick in *Fashioning the Frame: Boundaries, Dress and the Body* argue that "The prospect that dress may acquire the status of flesh as the body's deputy also intimates the possibility that if dress, as an artificial addition to the body, could be seen as the body's other, the body itself, as a symbolic category inconceivable outside representation, could be regarded as the other of dress" (116). Fashion can exist without a body, of course. Empty dresses hung in closets or on hangers in boutiques argue for such. But as fashion can be as much about movement as it is about construction, a body is a necessary aspect of fashion. My grandmother, working in the 1960s at a high-end department store to support her six children, was a model saleswoman, trying on the clothes for her customers so that they saw what it looked like on a body before they decided to put it on their bodies: a private catwalk for the elite of New Orleans society. It is no wonder that time and conversation with my stylish grandmother allowed me to see the importance of fashion.

For the Victorians, however, fashion became important for a number of interlaced reasons. The reading of fashion as a signal of class, gender, and morality is not unique to the Victorian era per se, but they fully embraced it and made it their own. In part due to the changes in class statuses—the flexibility of the middle class to rise from working middle class to higher becomes possible in the Victorian era thanks to the general rise of the middle class—Victorians looked to clothing to help communicate to what class a person belonged. Judith Flanders's *Inside the Victorian Home: A Portrait of Domestic Life in Victorian England* tells us that "Women were accustomed to 'reading' other women's clothes; novelists used details of dress as a language of status and identity that would be immediately understood. In a society with permeable class boundaries, clothes were important: every nuance was examined and decoded. It was not merely what was worn—how expensive it was, and where it was ready-made or made to measure—that mattered, but also when it was worn, and how it was worn" (293). More affordable fashions, a vigorous secondhand fashion trade, and the passing down of fashions from ladies of the house to their maids made this unreliable. Therefore, the telltale sign became manners, the *way* in which the dress was worn, that certain something that no one can define. She just *is* refined. A lady.

Further, the Victorian attention on morality heightened awareness of dress codes. The freeing empire waist gowns of the Regency era were too scandalous for the Victorians, who had wider and wider skirts with the crinoline in the 1850s and 1860s (also scandalous) and tighter and tighter skirts in the 1870s and 1880s (also scandalous), but it seemed that women's free movement became the moral test. A woman's place, according to Coventry Patmore's influential 1854 poem "The Angel in the House," was in the home with her family and children, and she certainly did not need ease of movement for the streets if she stayed home.

Of course, this is just not a feasible expectation for any woman who has to work for a living, and while Patmore's poem does not take into account the working-class woman (or, really, see her existence as important at all), these women too wore fashionable clothing. Many tracts of the nineteenth century spoke against servants dressing as their betters, to better learn to stay "in their place" and not have expectations of high society. While the nineteenth century may have middle-class women marrying rich men—Elizabeth Bennet, Jane Eyre—the real-life of Hannah Cullwick seems to be the only (albeit strangely) happy ending to this servant marrying upward narrative.

It may be no surprise to you, Reader, that one of the questions that plagues fashion scholars is rather a simple one: for whom do women dress? Who is the audience for elaborate fashions? Of course, for years, fashion and eroticism were intertwined (Valerie Steele, one of the renowned fashion scholars and curators, published the book entitled *Fashion and Eroticism*), and the assumption was entirely heterocentric, saying that women dressed to seduce, the implication being that women dressed to seduce men.

The problems write themselves in this case, as of course not all women are attracted to men, seemingly unfashionable women still find sexual partners, and, to be honest, the stereotype of men not knowing anything about fashion would ring true here.[17] There are questions about erogenous zones revealed or hidden by fabrics,[18] but the truth of the matter is simple: women dress for other women, including themselves. Sharon Marcus's *Between Women* reminds us that "Scholars have dismissed nineteenth-century dolls and fashion as mere tools for teaching women to become objects for men" and that "Victorian dolls and fashion iconography encouraged girls and women to desire images of femininity, without marking such desires as queer or lesbian" (9). The words Marcus uses here are important: dismissed, mere, objects, desire. Or, to make a more contemporary reference to women dressing or using fashion as a way to communicate with other women, consider the gender that usually compliments women on their clothing. Real bodies wearing real clothes communicate across boundaries of nation, sexuality, and intent; why then would it be any different in fiction?

To speak of fashion within novels is to claim something quite different indeed. Anne M. Buck asks, "Why then should we turn to fiction when we have fact? It would be unwise to rely on the evidence of fiction alone, but used together with the factual evidence the novelists' evidence may reveal the influences and ways of life which are expressed through dress"

(90). This belief that the textiles and the literature must be observed at the same time in order to fully understand the language of fashion and dress is at the core of my argument throughout this book. To see one with the other is to understand real bodies moving in spaces that influence the fictional bodies on the page. What then complicates this relationship is its proximity to nationalist ideology.

Fanny Douglas in *The Gentlewoman's Book of Dress* as late as 1895 spoke about the importance of national pride in fashion when she states, "Good dressing, like charity, should begin at home" (43). Looking at both the home, the domestic space of the family, and Home, the domestic space of England, allows us to contemplate the truth of Linda Colley's argument in "Britishness and Otherness: An Argument" that "Quite simply, we usually decide who we are by reference to who and what we are not" (311). These distinctions, as we will see, are operated on a fashionable level. Antony Easthope in *Englishness and National Culture* argues, "National unity, nation as unity, is an effect. It is an effect, first of all, of the process of collective identification with a common object which is accompanied by identification of individuals with each other" (22). As early as 1754, we can see discussions of women's nationalism bandied about in fashion magazines, determining the difference between the French and the English. "Mr. Town" in *The Connoisseur* argues, "Let the *French* ladies white wash and plaister their fronts, and lay on their colors with a trowel; but these dawbings of art are no more to be compared to the genuine glow of a *British* cheek, than the coarse streaks of the painter's brush can resemble the native veins of the marble" (as qtd. in Festa 32). These assumptions of genuineness among British women will be reiterated throughout the centuries, especially when in comparison to French women. Here, we see the comparison about cosmetics, but the comparisons are made in all aspects of the fashionable world: dress, cosmetics, accessories, society. French women are seen as imitative, whereas Englishwomen are too pure, too "genuine" to put on the airs and aspects the Frenchwomen do.[19]

Eliza Lynn Linton's 1868 essay "Nearing the Rapids" sees women as "the queens of society" who "fashion the manners and decide the standard of morality of that society" (378) but does not necessarily see this as a strength. She argues, "When the rule of woman has begun, and the men have to tail off behind the petticoat, we shall be more French than the French themselves, with irresponsible empresses pressing on disastrous wars, and peripatetic Louis Michels advocating loot and insurrection" (279). As Colley argues, nationalism is about seeing oneself in relation or opposition to another person or group. For Englishwomen, therefore, the alternative group is always the French. Lori Ann Loeb argues, "Exhortations to buy British or to champion the war effort [in advertising] were straightforward appeals to the emotional force of nationalism. They identify consumption with popular national goals" (153). To buy English-made products and fashions, and especially to ignore the fact that they originate in France, is for the nineteenth century, a true sign of nationalist pride.

We see this call for nationalist shopping in women's magazines of the time. Many fashions, as Sharon Marcus reminds us, originated in France, and it was French fashions that the English were admiring and purchasing. Even the gorgeous purple dress that graces the cover of the book you are holding in your hand is a blend of French and English: from the House of Worth, a Parisian boutique and fashion house, but designed by an Englishman, Charles Frederick Worth. But as we will see, changing French fashions to fit English sensibilities is an active objective of magazines. Karin J. Bohleke discusses the national changes of French fashion plates and notes, "*Godey's* produced its first 'Americanised' fashion plate in July 1846 and explained the differences between it and the original French in these vague terms: the plate is 'modified from the grossness of the French' and that 'our dresses are always those that a modest woman might wear.' Such will always be our rule—therefore our title of 'Paris Fashions Americanized'" (121).[20]

As it is now, the fashion industry for women is an incredibly successful and lucrative enterprise. Rachel Bowlby in *Carried Away: The Invention of Modern Shopping* even notes that "The department store is considered to be feminine, frivolous, French and fashionable" (9). The very concept of an enclosed space in which one can purchase anything one can think of is of course, French, but is brought to England through Selfridge's and, of course, Liberty's. Further, for those in charge of these fashionable shifts, Christopher Breward in "Femininity and Consumption: The Problem of the Late Nineteenth-Century Fashion Journal" argues that "Perhaps the most important instance of cultural intervention was the realization by publishers that feminine culture, or fashion, was a marketable commodity" (72). Middle-class women may not earn the money they spend, but they certainly spend it with enthusiasm, offering capitalists an entire gender to sway and entice with beautiful items, especially those that, like strawberries, are "good" and "English."[21]

Returning once again to those good English strawberries, I am reminded of Gaskell's Amazonian town, Cranford, and its army of middle-class impoverished spinsters operating happily in their world without men. It seems certain to me that the Cranfordians would understand the importance of nationalizing strawberries and see how important English strawberries would be to the health of the nation. Perhaps strawberries will change nationalities now that Brexit has occurred, but back in 2011, when I heard those two women discussing their importance, I confess I, too, wanted good English strawberries. So many things are coded still in England: Irish butter, Scottish preserves, Welsh cakes. So many of this originated in the Victorian era, it seems, and in Cranford, we see the importance of Englishness overwhelming the origins of items from France, like crinolines.

Chapters and the Structure of the Book

Understanding the usefulness of dress in the realities of everyday life, Victorian novelists utilize it in their fiction by presenting women concerned with dress and its national implications, or by manipulating the national implications of dress in order to influence readers' interpretations of characters. Whether playful or serious, gently mocking or completely sincere, many nineteenth-century novels present this concern over the expanding British Empire and the consequently contracting English nation by presenting characters continuously concerned with national distinctions. Hand in hand with concern over the expansion of the British Empire is the concern over the expansion of women's roles both in the home and in the public arena and women's increasing visibility in both places. This exposure of women becomes for the nineteenth century best defined through their outward presentation of self, and dress is vital in that self's establishment. As the three epigraphs that begin this introduction demonstrate, fashion and dress are for nineteenth-century women about preference: preference over with what to cover their bodies, over their outward presentations of real or fictional inner selves, and even over their allegiance to certain nationalist affiliations. Exploring these articles of women's clothing and, larger, women's concerns about and access to the fashionable arena in the novels of the period—through dress, through social standing, through prestige, and even through the construction and production of articles of clothing—is to see the concerns of the nation writ large in the entertainment of the nation. These concerns of fashion and nation are concerns of the general populace, of the people of England, of the women of England, written by some of the most popular novelists of Victorian England, through the vehicle of enjoyment and, as we understand the Victorian novel today, through the vehicle of social and political commentary as well.

The structure of this book is thematic. While the chapters in their entirety cover the Victorian period, they do not do so in chronological order. My research into discussions of fashion of the nineteenth century proves to me that these discussions were similar across the scope of time. That is to say, discussions of anti-Frenchness in *Cranford* in the middle of the century are the same that we see in anti-Frenchness in *Diana of the Crossways* in the late 1800s. Concerns over women's toilette and improper dressing, including discussions of corsetry, happen throughout the century. Further, this book is concerned with both novels and textiles, and as such, each chapter will read both novels and textiles. Each chapter will, as its focal point, center on an object of fashion from one of several archives to provide a touchstone of fashion for the chapter. I am deeply indebted to *The Dress Detective* as well as the 2017 National Endowment for the Humanities Institute I attended on American Material Culture in Nineteenth-Century New York. Both of these experiences—reading the book, attending the Institute—helped to cement my reading of nontextual objects. Further, I am grateful for the curators and archivists who helped me throughout the years since I began this work in reading fashion and nationalism; they are thanked in the acknowledgments of this book, but I felt that their work should not go unmentioned here in discussions of methods and theories.

Also of note are two distinctions: nationalism versus patriotism and fashion versus dress. In my discussions of nationalism, I will include instances of patriotism, although the two are essentially different. Nationalism is, in my estimation, adherence to a specific mindset or ideal of a nation, while patriotism is demonstrable pride in that nation. Further complicating these distinctions are the changes inherent in establishing the British Empire. As for fashion and dress, dress is contained within fashion, but not all dress is fashionable. When I speak of fashion, I speak of clothing with some sense of style and modernity. But there is fashionability in being antifashionable, as we see with the Amazons in *Cranford*.

Finally, it must be said, that because of the nature of the novels I'm exploring, the majority of the clothing I will explore will be that belonging to middle- and upper-class white women. There are rare instances of nonwhite or working-class women in Victorian literature—*Vanity Fair*'s Miss Swartz, for example, or the factory girls in Elizabeth Gaskell's *Mary Barton*. But it is only when I discuss historical persons, especially those involved with the British suffrage movement, that we see the true face of the empire revealed: one that is decidedly nonwhite. While women had little political power in England, the women of the empire had even less, colonized by the English into subjects considered inferior to the English by the English. Only recently do we see the true multiracial face of England, in the figure of Meghan Markle, the Duchess of Sussex, and given her and Prince Harry's decision to retire from royal life, we can see that the concerns of English versus non-English, white versus nonwhite, are unfortunately alive in the twenty-first century just as they were in the nineteenth.

Chapter One, " 'That Wicked Paris': Elizabeth Gaskell Fashions the Good Englishwoman," argues that the crises of authenticity sparked by the expanding British Empire and increasing contact with France often were articulated through fictional and nonfictional discussions of fashion. As Englishwomen were figured as symbols of nation, attention to their presentations of self, and therefore of Englishness, became anxious attention to their fashion choices. The minute details of dress—petticoats, turbans, crinolines, and fabrics—became a particular point of discussion for Sarah Stickney Ellis, Eliza Lynn Linton, and Elizabeth Gaskell, and these pieces of ensemble were read for national as well as personal origin and allegiance. This chapter argues that Gaskell's *Cranford* (1853) offers a microcosmic view of the larger English concern over the empire's and France's influence on the people of England through Englishwomen's fashionable choices. Through its discussions of shawls, crinolines, and red umbrellas, Gaskell's novel demonstrates that everyday items of domesticity speak not only of the concerns of women but also of the concerns of nation.

Chapter Two, "William Thackeray's Fashionable Humbugs and Unfashionable Darlings: Consuming National Distinctions of Dress," argues that the presence of foreign women and foreign ideals in English settings—those of place and those of people—complicated England's ability to define itself through the symbolic figure of its women and their outward displays of fashion. The English and their clothing became more cosmopolitan simultaneously, beginning with the Napoleonic Wars and continuing through the technological advancement of the nineteenth century. As the British Empire expanded, England itself contracted, and the nation attempted to define its women as natural beauties in opposition to the supposedly artificial beauties of Frenchwomen as an attempt to claim superiority of character, beauty, and belief in its women. William Thackeray's *Vanity Fair* (1848) presents the dichotomy of Amelia Sedley and Becky Sharp, English and French, respectively, natural and artificial, respectively, and "Fashionable Humbugs" argues that Amelia and Becky's differences are articulated through the presentation of their fashion choices in order to demonstrate their similarities. As fashion is artificial, so, too, is beauty, and both nationality and "natural beauty" can be artificially constructed, regardless of national origin.

Chapter Three, " 'The Will and Pleasure of Women': The Feminine Love of Fashion in George Eliot's *Middlemarch*," explores fashion and dress as arenas of power for women during a time when attention to fashionable accoutrements would suggest immorality, selfishness, and a lack of character, and thus the opposite of how middle-class England wanted to define its standards of femininity and womanhood. George Eliot's *Middlemarch* (1871–1872) not only sympathizes with but also celebrates a woman's love and appreciation of dress. By rejecting the common stereotype of a fashionable woman as selfish and vain and thus presenting the commendable and selfless Dorothea Brooke as fashionable and fashionably aware, Eliot's novel argues that fashion is beneficial to nineteenth-century women's lives. It also argues for the importance of fashion for Englishwomen and against the belief that a love of fashion signals the antithesis of Englishness.

Chapter Four, " 'Now She's All Hat and Ideas': Fashioning the British Suffrage Movement," notes the late nineteenth-century's attention to politicized dress. I argue that as suffragettes paid particular attention to the outward markers of self and femininity, they did so both to claim participation in nation and also to maintain association with traditional femininity in order to legitimize their efforts to an audience potentially hostile to their cause. Through a discussion of specific articles of national dress such as the Lancashire clogs and shawl or the Scottish kilt and a discussion of H. G. Wells's *Ann Veronica* (1909), this chapter argues that women's participation in nation building and nation maintenance not only manipulated traditional gender and national roles but also adhered to those roles to prove that national allegiance and social transgression were synonymous and that characters could be both politically and fashionably capable.

By the end of this book, in a final discussion of nationalism in wedding dresses from a queen, two duchesses, and a princess (conclusion, "To Have and to Wear: National Distinctions of Dress in Royal Weddings"), we will see that our discussion of fashion and English nationalism does not end when Queen Victoria's reign ends or the Edwardian era begins or when women succeed in fighting for the vote. Rather, it continues today, in the beautiful wedding gowns of Victoria, Kate Middleton, Princess Eugenie, and Meghan Markle. Each woman chose specific items of nationalist display to present themselves to the world, aligning their fashions with the countries they love.

And each woman was dressing *for* a nation.

"That Wicked Paris"

Elizabeth Gaskell Fashions the Good Englishwoman

Figure 1.1. Thomson's Empress Crinoline in Red. *Source:* Courtesy of the London Museum. Used with permission.

What strikes a modern observer first is how small it is, this beautiful red crinoline housed in the London Museum's fashion archives. When one speaks of crinolines, one remembers how big they were reported to be, mocked in the presses for the sheer audacity of allowing women to take up space.[1] Labeled by fashion tracts as "monstrosities" ("The Dangers of Crinoline" 3), women who wore the popular cage crinoline were accused of pushing children into fires and men into rivers with the size of their skirts. There was no forgiveness for a Victorian woman who occupied public space, it seems. And the crinoline was made to occupy space: it required larger skirts, for women to go through doorways sideways, and any means of awkwardness when embarking on a carriage ride. Further, it was dangerous to England not because of its size or cumbersomeness—in fact, many women remarked that the crinoline freed them from the oppression of several petticoats—but because it originated in France. Terri Hasseler notes, "Crinoline's foreign origins in France made it a special subject of ridicule for its excessiveness, expensiveness and invasiveness" (131). The word *invasiveness* is important here, because we see the crinoline occupying the role of social and national invader. It was different; it was feminine; it took up space; it was French. "The Dangers of Crinoline" even uses nationalistic language to plead against the crinoline, stating, "Oh daughters of England! oh mothers! oh wives! ponder upon these bitter truths, and cease to make yourselves a prey to vanity, and the martyrs of fashion!" (6). Like many fashion or moralistic tracts of the time, "The Dangers of Crinoline" appeals directly to a woman's sense of nationalism and Englishness to stop her fashionable madness.

The *Oxford English Dictionary* defines *crinoline* as:

> A stiffened petticoat or underskirt made with this material, designed to support the skirts of a woman's dress; (hence) a rigid petticoat worn for this purpose, lined with, or consisting of, a framework of some other material, as whalebone, steel hoops, etc.; a hoop petticoat. Though the crinoline (which might reach 2m in diameter) enjoyed greatest popularity in the mid 19th cent., a smaller version may still be worn as part of a formal outfit, under an evening gown or wedding dress.

The origins of the crinoline are, of course, French, as many popular items of fashion are, but the crinoline experienced a change when it came to England, in expectation, and, as we will see with Elizabeth Gaskell's works, in construction as well. Perhaps because it was French, it allowed women to take up space. But when one speaks of Victorians, of the people of the nineteenth century, one must remember that they were, on average, smaller than we are now. Women, in reality, then, took up *less* space. It only goes to support the reason why this crinoline is positively *tiny*. The accession number is 46.33/12/LW.COS.U.P4.7., and it is labeled as "Thomson's Empress crinoline, red," with dates ranging from 1861 to 1865. There are twelve hoops down the front of the crinoline, but only eight hoops down the back. The hoops are held together with metal fasteners, with seven strips of fabric working downward. There are eyelet fasteners where the fabric meets the shorter hoops, and the original label is still on the item, marked with a crown and labeled, "Thomson's Empress," with an A in the middle. The waistband is reinforced with red material sewn on top of the muslin with black thread, down the back where the buttocks would be. This item was worn, because we can see the stains on it, the places where the threads have popped out.

We should also ask, why red? Red is a color one cannot escape from. It cries for attention and wants to be seen. A person does not wear red and blend into the background, playing wallflower at the local ball. But this is a crinoline, technically underwear, and it is red. Who would see this? The wearer would know it was red and perhaps it would give her some courage as she stepped, trepidatious, onto a ballroom floor. Maybe passersby would get a glimpse of this red crinoline's bottom hoops as she walked up stairs to the ladies' retiring room. Her lover would see it, surely, as well as her maid. As would the proprietor who sold it to her, this private, intimate thing. And now, I have seen it, as a very private thing is put on public display for archivists, historians, and me.

The conflation of private and public was a reality in the Victorian era, as the so-called separate spheres were not as separate as Victorian society pretended them to be. What happened in the home was writ large for the nation, the little "h" of home standing in for the big "H" of Home, of England, of Britain, and, therefore, of empire. These gendered homes, then, women for the domestic sphere and men for the national, were conflated as well. To believe that women had no place in the nation, and, further, in the empire, is to believe the truth of the separate spheres that were, as we have come to see, not so separate after all. Even early in the period, long before this crinoline was thought of or made or bought, writers were conflating the domestic home with the domestic home front and urging women to consider their actions for both queen and country.

In her 1839 conduct tract *The Women of England*, Sarah Stickney Ellis argues that despite her growing concern over the lagging morality of her countrywomen, and therefore of England, she still believes that "the women of England are not surpassed by those of any other country for their clear perception of the right and the wrong of common and familiar things, for their reference to principle in the ordinary affairs of life, and for their united maintenance of that social order, sound integrity, and domestic peace, which constitute the foundation of all that is most valuable in the society of our native land" (36). While Ellis notes that "the national characteristics of England are the perpetual boast of her patriotic sons" (9), she lays the foundation of the nation at the feet of its women rather than its men, as women are the maintainers of "social order, sound integrity, and domestic peace." For Ellis, as for so many Victorian writers, women's place lies not only in the home, a physical place of residence, but also in the Home, an ideology based on domestic pursuits and concerns particular to English society.[2] These domestic pursuits, "the home comforts, and fireside virtues for which [England] is so justly celebrated," are "one of the noblest features in [England's] national character" and more often than not are regarded "as within the compass of a woman's understandings and the province of a woman's pen" (9–10). In writing her conduct tract, Ellis takes up her own "woman's pen" and defines the national character of England, instructing Englishwomen on what it is to be English.

Ellis's concern with the Englishness of her nation's women reiterates itself throughout the instructional and fictional literature of the period; Victorian England suffers under a crisis of national definition. As new peoples and ideas arrive in England from the burgeoning and expanding empire, this crisis of national definition and, indeed, of national authenticity, is more often than not debated through women and their roles in nationhood. Ellis and other Victorian women writers, such as Elizabeth Gaskell, take up their pens to encourage women to conquer what they see as the flagging morality and pretenses at sophistication fracturing the nineteenth-century middle class. They use scenes of home and its domestic, feminine concerns, such as fashion, as microcosmic parallels for larger domestic concerns: those of the nation itself.

Elizabeth Gaskell's 1853 novel *Cranford* presents a nearly all-female community that is responsible for creating, establishing, and maintaining the culture and morality of its provincial town. As the Cranfordians are women and therefore concerned with so-called feminine things, fashion, dress, and shopping become the markers of nationality and the signals of cultural cohesion by which the Cranfordians form their inclusive English community. England's cultural and social war with France, especially as it is represented in Gaskell's novel, is in itself a microcosm of a larger crisis of national authenticity; "France" and "French fashions" personify foreignness for England during its time of empire and expansion, and women are charged with the protection of the symbolic borders that separate England from France and thus define Englishness. This protection, more often than not, occurs within the fashionable arena, as it does in *Cranford*.

Elizabeth Gaskell's novels *Cranford* and *North and South* and her shorter work, "The Cage at Cranford," represent the Victorian woman writer's struggle to ascertain women's role within nationhood, particularly in how women navigate the social and domestic arenas. Fashion is both public and private; it conceals and reveals the articulation of personal and national beliefs. Gaskell's focus on Englishwomen in her novels enfolds discussions of shopping, finance, and matters of the heart within the larger concerns of her nation, namely concerns of consumption, of economics, and of domesticity, to argue that fashion and dress enable these fictional female characters to find an arena in which they can articulate their understandings of a world that would, by all accounts, be denied to them. By presenting women who manipulate common perceptions of fashion to their specific requirements and for their own means, Gaskell offers a view of Englishwomen who are in constant awareness of the public reading of their private fashionable choices. When Gaskell's characters alter, wear, or discuss foreign fashions (the turban, the Kashmir shawl, the crinoline) to accommodate their English climate, social strata, or national expectations for modesty, they are, in fact, actively scripting the very definition of what it means to be a successful Englishwoman.

The Preservation of Englishness:
Gaskell Scripts the Good Englishwoman

In her continuous attempts to define the national character of her country, Sarah Stickney Ellis devotes particular attention not only to actions but also to signals of nationalism.[3] For Ellis, an Englishwoman's loyalty to her country is evident in the services she performs and the image she presents. Ellis argues that if a woman, despite all appearances of accomplishments and outward displays of finery, were to reveal "underneath her graceful drapery, the soiled hem, the tattered frill," those private items of dress that call to mind "her dressing room, her private habits," then those soiled and tattered items most likely would reflect "her inner mind, where, it is almost impossible to believe that the same want of order and purity does not prevail" (96). For Ellis, that soiled hem of a dress, therefore, indicates a soiled and slatternly mind; this revelation of the private calls to mind other secret, private things. Yet by noticing that soiled hem and thereby judging women by their outward appearances, Ellis is emphasizing the very thing on which she warns her countrywomen not to place importance: fashion. For Ellis, the attention a woman devotes to her dress distracts her from fulfilling her role as the daughter, wife, or mother of her country's men; yet a disregard for dress—that soiled hem of which Ellis warns—signals disregard for the continuous representation of true and good Englishness through neat and pretty dress. In the framework that Ellis creates, Englishwomen are judged both by their outward appearances and the very attention they pay to those outward appearances; there is, it seems, no happy medium between the two.

Nowhere, then, are women better judged as spectacles than in the arena of fashion. Fashion, defined for these purposes as stylish, trendy, and ornamental dress, so often is viewed as the outward marker of a woman's inner self and thereby becomes the signal of a woman's worth. Diana Crane argues that the visibility of clothing and its conspicuous consumption construct an immediate identity in the social world (1). Fashion's direct recognition by its viewers and its ability to be "read" indicate a language of dress that few, if any, can escape. Crane argues that dress, its fabrics, its accessories, and its use of color and style convey a recognizable class status (50) but that status is, ultimately, completely artificial and immediately recognizable. As fashion articulates a language of class status, it also articulates a language of nationality because many nations possess what they deem "national dress"; their citizens are therefore accustomed to reading fashion and dress as nationally charged.[4] As advancements in technology and marketing allow a democracy of dress in the nineteenth century, corresponding crises of authenticity, both class and national, come into play. The attention women pay to their toilette becomes more than the distraction from patriotism that Ellis suggests; instead as Englishwomen are read as middle class or not, as moral or not, as neat and pretty or not, they are read as English or not, as patriotic or not. As England expands its empire and thus redefines the meaning of *British*, it becomes even more important to confirm and support the ideal of "true" Englishness as the nation encounters these crises of authenticity.

I begin with Sarah Stickney Ellis because she marks the beginning of Victoria's reign and writes of ideologies that will come to represent the best of the Victorians, to the Victorians themselves. Ellis's early manners text can be seen as a prototype for several of the manners texts to follow, including those that deal with women and fashion. But Ellis is also representative of a line of thinking that declares that the women of the nation, and not its men, are responsible for the nation's successes and failures. Tamar Meyer argues that in many nationalistic narratives, "the nation is virtually always feminized and characterized as in need of protection; women are figured as the biological and cultural reproducers of the nation" (10). While this may be true of many nationalistic narratives, *The Women of England* differs because it focuses on women as the protectors of the nation rather than symbols of the femininity that needs to be protected. When Ellis charges her readers with the plea "You have deep responsibilities, you have urgent claims; a nation's moral wealth is in your keeping" (13), she is placing the moral protection of a nation directly in the hands of its women and thus is seeing them as active protectors of nationalism and not just its biological or cultural reproducers. The men of England may physically protect its borders and answer the imperial call for the expansion of the empire, but the women of England preserve its integrity, its mission, and, in truth, its ideals.

Elizabeth Gaskell's novels often present women concerned with fashion—its manufacturing, its social resonance, its cultural capital—but in most of her works, these concerns are superseded by, indeed, sacrificed to, representations of sexuality, innocence, and seduction. *Mary Barton* (1848), *Ruth* (1853), and *Wives and Daughters* (1864–1866) all present the seductive power of fabric, and the connection drawn between seamstresses and moral issues. But in *Cranford*, Gaskell instead uses dress and accoutrements to demonstrate how the shifting socioeconomic landscape of England works to define its people and its identity and the subsequent effects they have on the women native to the land. Drawing on the fashions of the 1830s, the time in which *Cranford* is set, Gaskell presents fashionable items, such as the Indian shawls that are brought to England from locations throughout the British Empire, as part of the English home. The British Empire's advances into foreign nations inevitably bring foreign goods and people back to the seat of imperialism, England, and the concerns over the possible contamination of the English home through these foreign objects makes it crucial for the objects themselves to be seen as harmless. These objects thus must be domesticated and made suitable for good Englishwomen's homes. Cannon Schmitt posits that provincial novels like *Cranford* "domesticate the imperial, naturalizing territorial aggression within the provincial settings of realistic narrative" (16). Underneath the domestic talk of tea trays, lace, turbans, and shawls of Cranford's female citizens, referred to as Amazons, lies a disturbing threat of imminent transformation and infiltration of the English countryside by outside, foreign forces, represented by the very fashionable items for which the people so long.

In calling the women of Cranford "Amazons," Gaskell offers her female characters participation in the aggressive maintenance and defense of their homes. This characterization is a rather sly one on the part of Gaskell, however, in that these Amazons aggressively maintain and defend their homes through manners, parties, and other so-called trivial feminine concerns. The designation "Amazon," then, is twofold: it offers a serious glimpse into the importance of "feminine concerns" in the construction of the town, and thus nation and empire, and it offers comic relief in the visual fantasy of the elderly women of Cranford as warrior women. As the Cranford Amazons begin to notice the changing landscape, they attempt to protect their ways of life against the encroaching ravages of time and change and against the "territorial aggression" that is at the heart of the British Empire.

Often invoked as a novel of nostalgia, innocence, and "pastoral charm" (Cass 418), *Cranford* seems to represent the best, and last, of the small English town. Jeffrey Cass argues that Gaskell's attention to the seemingly insignificant and quirky details of life in the town, which both he and Gaskell refer to as "Cranfordisms," are in fact representations of the Cranfordian women's desperate attempt to cling to an era gone by. This bygone era—pre–mass transportation and pre–mass consumption—evokes a nostalgic simplicity that belies the drastic shifts in culture that occur throughout the novel. Captain Brown's death both by train and by modern literature, Miss Matty's bankruptcy, and the infiltration of Cranford by turban-wearing Englishmen masquerading as Italians counter the Cranfordians' disregard for technological, social, cultural, and fashionable shifts taking place throughout the novel's timeframe. As Cranford seemingly resists change to its fashions, its people, and its pastoral and innocent way of life, it is in fact participating in the rapid changes to the same that are spreading across England. Cranford's desperate hold on its nostalgic charm cannot protect it from outside forces. Instead, it becomes a facsimile of encapsulation; Cranford, like many small towns across the nation, cannot withstand the assault of modernization. This modernization is a direct result of colonial progress, the vast advances in technology, and the shifts in gender politics that drive Gaskell's novel. There are few middle-class men in Cranford because many of them are dead, abroad, or consumed with military obligations.[5] Cranford is changing, despite its best efforts: the town would not be so wholly female if the empire was not so wholly in need of able-bodied men.

Like William Thackeray's *Vanity Fair* (1848), *Cranford* presents the effects of empire on nations and their peoples not through detailed discussions of invading military forces but rather through scenes that instead deal almost exclusively with "the ladies, and the baggage" (Thackeray 346). Both novels understand that to see the results of war and conquering armies, one must not look to the scene of war but instead to the women and their effects left behind. Thackeray's novel accounts for its domestic setting by arguing, "We do not claim to rank among the military novelists. Our place is with the non-combatants" (346), while Gaskell's novel accounts for the transience of men with a subtle warning. Mary Smith, the narrator, begins her tale:

> In the first place, Cranford is in possession of the Amazons; all the holders of houses, above a certain rent, are women. If a married couple come to settle in the town, somehow the gentleman disappears; he is either fairly frightened to death by being the only man in the Cranford evening parties, or he is accounted for by being with his regiment, his ship, or closely engaged in business all the week in the great neighbouring commercial town of Drumble, distant only twenty miles on a railroad. In short, whatever does become of the gentlemen, they are not at Cranford. What could they do if they were there? (1)

This introduction serves as a warning and, to a certain extent, a threat to England and its empire through the ambiguous description of the disappearing gentleman, as well as the sly suggestion that he is "frightened to death" in a female-exclusive social world—and that the women are actively engaged in the frightening. But in setting the scene of her novel with such a colorful and explicit introduction, Gaskell also implicates the role that progress plays in eliminating men from the English countryside. The men are "accounted for" in their regiment, on their ship, or in their commercial enterprises readily accessible by rail. The novel notes that there is no longer a need for men in Cranford, for indeed, "What could they do if they were there?" and argues that the sacrifice of men to the greater technological and imperial good will result in female exclusivity. In short, the town is going to the women.

By establishing female exclusivity, *Cranford* reiterates its concern with feminine affairs; because the town is in possession of the Amazons, the town must be concerned with Amazonian things. And as fashion is relegated to women because it is so often marketed and directed specifically to women, Cranford's interest in fashion is seen as a "natural" feminine interest. The first discussions of fashion in *Cranford* concern cultural belatedness. The townswomen's seeming obliviousness to fashion trends would be laughable if that obliviousness were not actually a conscious refusal of change. After declaring Cranford an Amazon town, Mary tells us that the "last gigot, the last tight and scanty petticoat in wear in England, was seen in Cranford—and seen without a smile" (2). The gigot, also known as the leg-of-mutton sleeve, and the small petticoats are the fashions of the previous generation, one even Gaskell calls "The Last Generation of England" in her precursor to the novel. The excuse given in the novel for this lack of fashionability is "elegant economy," and because the majority of the town exists in "general but unacknowledged poverty," pinching pennies becomes a fashion in itself. It is also the result of pure contrariness (3).[6] Despite the fact that their "dress is very independent of fashion," the women of Cranford wonder, "What does it signify how we dress here at Cranford, where everybody knows us?" when they are home, and "What does it signify how we dress here, where nobody knows us?" when they are away (2). These statements suggest not that Cranford's citizens are oblivious to fashion, but rather that they are quite conscious of it, enough to recognize their "independence" in dress and their decision to ignore current trends. In fact, Mary's note that "the materials of their clothes are, in general, good and plain" (2) suggests that the Amazons do desire to maintain some modicum of fashionability. To be fashionable in nineteenth-century England is not only to be aware of the latest fashion trends but also to wear good material. This access to "materials . . . good and plain" separates the Amazons from lower-class women, who may have access to dress patterns but would not have access, certainly, to the expensive fabrics with which to make dresses themselves. Further, Mary's observation proves that the Amazons understand the implications good dress has in society. The citizens of Cranford have turned their "elegant economy" of dress and the "cultural belatedness" of their fashions into a fashion statement of their own: quirky and independent, albeit dowdy and quaint, yet always middle class.

Mary Smith faithfully records this resistance to change and presents a sympathetic, though at times witty and gently mocking, view of the Amazons' plight. When she presents an image of a tiny spinster walking to church under a large red silk umbrella, she asks the reader, "Have you any red silk umbrellas in London?" (2). This question serves three purposes in the narration. First, it offers a dichotomy between the charmingly unfashionable Cranfordians and the more sophisticated reading public in London. Second, it proves Mary's know-how and innate sense of fashion; she knows that such things are not seen in London and are therefore woefully out of style. And third, it illuminates the difference between Mary and the Cranfordians and notes that she exists both as a theoretical outsider who infiltrates Cranford and as an accepted member of the community. Rowena Fowler reminds us of Mary's in-betweenness; she notes that Mary, in her existence between Cranford and "the nearby manufacturing town of Drumble, is sometimes too influenced by the matter-of-factness of the latter to appreciate the roundabout logic of the former" (720). But it is this very in-betweenness that allows Mary not only to describe the details of the Amazonian town but also to nudge Cranford toward its modernization. In fact, Mary often prompts change in Cranford: she knows the shifting fashions in dining and clothing, she helps Miss Matty open her tea shop, and she brings Peter, Miss Matty's brother, home to England from India. In this sense, then, Mary becomes an agent of modernization who helps to assimilate Cranford not only to the larger cultural landscape of an England changed by foreign goods and ideas but also to the technological, fashionable, and social shifts that have begun to find their ways into the town.

The understanding of "good and plain" fashions as a marker of respectability and morality is intrinsically connected to both nationalism and class; as the nineteenth century continues on, it is certainly the middle class who is most invested in these markers. Sarah Stickney Ellis urges her readers not to aspire to be the women who dress above and beyond their station. She offers such an example to her readers and notes that if the woman "had been dressed in a plain substantial costume, corresponding with her mind and habits, she might have been known at once, and respected for what she really was,—a rational, independent, and valuable member of society" (102). To see the social worth in dressing in correspondence with one's social class is particularly relevant for Ellis's intended audience, those women whose marriages or family fortunes offer a chance of mobility within the strata of the middle class, but it also represents a larger concern for nineteenth-century England and its textile industry. Dating back to the Renaissance, the English understanding of textiles' ability to communicate national information about its wearer gains particular prominence as the British textile industry expands.[7] As late as 1895, Mrs. Fanny Douglas argues for Englishwomen to "encourage home industries" (37) because while foreign textiles may be fashionably desirable, "every year . . . our manufacturers are producing finer designs, lovelier tones, and more beautiful qualities than before, and some of the brocades that issue from Spitalfields rival in exquisite taste the finest fabrics of the past" (38). Texts such as Mrs. Douglas's that urged their English audiences to purchase and wear domestic fabrics can be seen in part as an economic incentive to help the burgeoning cotton industry in Northern England.

Support for the "home industries" begins not as Mrs. Douglas suggests, in a fervor of national pride, but rather in the accessibility of fabrics produced in England or Scotland. Suzanne Daly's article "Spinning Cotton: Domestic and Industrial Novels" informs us that a "profound shift in the vexed relationship between East India Company traders and English textile manufacturers occurred as the race to imitate domestically the colors, textures, and patterns of Indian cloth gave rise to a series of technological innovations that were retrospectively named the industrial revolution" (273). The rise of cotton mills in Northern England, particularly in the Manchester fictionally referenced as Drumble in Gaskell's novel, worked to produce textiles that surpassed Indian textiles in at least affordability if not popularity. Indian cloth, however, was still the more fashionable choice among those who could afford it. Throughout the nineteenth century, the association of foreign textiles with foreign virtues becomes writ large as the association of women's foreign fashion trends with their countries of origin. As so much of the fashionable discourse of the nineteenth century surrounds the moral revelations that come with a woman's choice in dress, a woman's choice of foreign rather than domestic garments becomes problematic when the dual life of foreign textiles is considered: they are "good" because they are well made, but they are ultimately "foreign," which carries the weight of all that the word implies to a nineteenth-century English audience. Supporting "home industries" becomes particularly important, as it offers a chance to wear "good and plain" materials: "good" because they are English, and "plain" because they are not overly decorated with patterns like many of the Indian cottons. To dissuade such confusions, foreign textiles must be rewritten so that their representations are staunchly English. Much of this rewriting occurs at the manufacturing stage itself, as textile factories in Northern England and Scotland spend most of the first half of the nineteenth century re-creating foreign fashions for domestic audiences.[8]

The suggestion of foreignness in Gaskell's novel—always hinted at but never crassly discussed—emphasizes the nineteenth-century fascination with the intrusion of the foreign into the domestic. To read this fascination through the lens of fashion, and to see it become, at times, fear, is to understand that nineteenth-century England believed itself to be constantly on the brink of the "invasion" of foreignness: of people, of culture, and of material items. Miss Matty's brother, Peter, is expelled from Cranford and, while he doesn't come back because he fears his father's wrath, even if he did, he would be assumed to be one of those men who have nothing to do in Cranford; it can offer nothing to a young man such as himself. And, like so many other such men without recourse or opportunity, Peter enlists in the Navy. Miss Matty tells Mary, "He had made his way to Liverpool; and there was war then; and some of the king's ships lay off the mouth of the Mersey; and they were only too glad to have a fine likely boy such as him (five foot nine he was) come to offer himself" (56). Miss Matty's language is one of regret and longing for the loss of her brother; it is also patriotic and reverential. She speaks of war, and king's ships, and of the offering, or, perhaps in this case, the sacrifice of a young boy "they were only too glad to have." Peter is caught up in this nationalistic fever, as well, as his letter home to his mother indicates. His language is naïvely expectant about war and filled with patriotic platitudes: "Mother! we may go into battle. I hope we shall, and lick those French" (57). But Peter's mother, rather than Peter, dies, and the day after her death, "came a parcel for her from India—from her poor boy. It was a large, soft white India shawl, with just a little narrow border all round; just what my mother would have liked" (58). The importance of this shawl is not in the giving of it, but rather in its cultural resonance. Peter does not merely send "just what [his] mother would have liked," but rather what all mothers would have liked: the symbolic return of the prodigal son, now wealthy and influential, who brings with him items of conquest and foreign nations. In the nineteenth century, the India shawl was often a gift given to female family members upon return from the East[9]; Peter, not yet at the conclusion of his military career, sends it while still away.

Like so many items of clothing in the nineteenth century, this Indian shawl is more than a fashionable accessory: it is a symbol of English prowess through its representation of the British Empire and the colonization of the East. Further, possession of such shawls is an assurance of respectability for Englishwomen; the price, accessibility, and quality of India shawls, particularly those made in the region of Kashmir, guarantee that only the wealthy can afford them.[10] Contemporary Victorian magazines reinforce the shawl's popularity in Britain and its market value in the world of fashion. *The Englishwoman's Domestic Magazine* of October 1870 notes that "Shawls are daily resuming their forever importance in the world of *elegantes*, and we must all have an Indian shawl if we would avoid the unlucky fate of the unfortunate lady who is confined to the house when it is windier than usual, because her shawl is not Indian" (qtd. in Chaudhuri 234). The language of this passage assumes a familiar reader, one who could or would afford a true Indian shawl, and, further, offers the fashionable imperative the shawl hopes for. The fact that the women "must all have an Indian shawl" drives the piece; even if a woman did not want a shawl before, she would now. But the passage also implies the mobility the shawl affords to Victorian women. The shawl acts as a buffer between a woman's body and the elements, certainly; it is cold out and a shawl would protect a woman from the cold. The author suggests that without the shawl, a woman would be exposed both to the elements and to the prying eyes of the fashionable "*elegantes*." Without an *Indian* shawl, warmer and more practical for English falls and winters, a woman's health would be in more danger. Underneath the seemingly practical fashion advice, however, is the domestic imperative that the shawl protects the private from the public and allows the private to appear in public at all. The active gaze of the public audience that would confine a woman to her home "because her shawl is not Indian" denotes the shawl as a necessary article of clothing.

Fashion demands the shawl's authenticity; in order to be fashionable, one must own an original Kashmir. By owning shawls made in India, Victorian women participated in the global marketplace. They consumed foreign objects and gained a sense of exoticism in the process. The Kashmir shawl occupies a liminal space in England; because of its visibility and its foreign design, it is both public and exotic, and because of its connection to the body and its attractiveness in the domestic arena, it is both private and English. Suzanne Daly remarks that such shawls "are ubiquitous in the domestic novels of the time where . . . they function at once as a marker of respectable English womanhood and as magic and mysterious 'oriental' garments" (238).[11] The giving and possessing of the shawl, then, become signifiers of respectable Englishness for both its wearer and its bearer: for the man, it represents his part in his nation's conquest and management of foreign lands, and for the woman, the class position and global awareness provided to her by successful male family members. When a man brought back the shawl from India to England, he proclaimed his reinstatement into English society. Daly notes, "Thus the shawl becomes a kind of ritual of casting-off for the returning man—he restores himself to England and to Englishness" (248). For Peter, the shawl represents his accomplishments as an English gentleman. Peter's gift of the shawl is an attempt to restore his legacy; the gift is for his mother, but its arrival should bear significance to the Cranford community at large. Their "functioning at once as exotic foreign artifacts and as markers of proper Englishness" (Daly 237) are taken one step further when the shawls enter the English home. They become markers of proper English masculinity and of proper English femininity for both Peter and his mother.

Perhaps the most famous example of the India shawl in Gaskell's work is its cameo appearance in a conversation within the first chapter of her 1854–1855 novel, *North and South*. Aunt Shaw discusses Edith's trousseau with Mrs. Gibson and notes the heirloom quality of these precious items: "I have spared no expense in her trousseau. . . . She has all the beautiful Indian shawls and scarfs [*sic*] the General gave to me, but which I shall never wear again" (9). Although the shawls are handed down, they are not considered castoffs. Their expense and significance in Victorian society warrant that Edith's trousseau is very well stocked indeed. Edith's mother is not only passing down important family artifacts but solidifying her daughter's wealth and class position as well.[12] The shawl's function as a symbol of wealth is most notably seen in Mrs. Gibson's next statement about her own daughter: "Helen had set her heart upon an Indian shawl, but really when I found what an extravagant price was asked, I was obliged to refuse her. She will be quite envious when she hears of Edith having Indian shawls" (9). The implication of the Gibsons' lower economic status is evident; while Helen has her heart set on just one shawl and is refused, Edith will be in possession of several.

When Margaret is asked to bring the shawls and model them for her aunt and her friend, she is transformed by them into "a princess" (11). The association with the royal court—and, more generally, with royalty—is one of empire and colonization as it brings to mind Queen Victoria and her title as Empress of India. When "Margaret went down laden with shawls, and snuffing up their spicy Eastern smell" (11), Gaskell evokes the origin of the garments by presenting their very foreignness. They smell not of the English home in which they preside but rather of the place of their origin. The "spicy Eastern smell" is a physical sense that invades Margaret's body; the scent travels into her, and once she dons the shawls, her transformation into this foreign-draped "princess" is complete. As Margaret stands "quite silent and passive, while her aunt adjusted the draperies" (11), she is moved around bodily to best display the garments. As she is, "she caught a glimpse of herself in the mirror over the chimney-piece, and smiled at her own appearance there—the familiar features in the usual garb of a princess" (11). The shawls are better suited for "Margaret's tall, finely made figure" than for the cousin for whom they are intended, and Margaret's black mourning gown "set off the long beautiful folds of the gorgeous shawls that would have half-smothered Edith" (11). By wearing these shawls, Margaret becomes both the proper Englishwoman displaying the spoils of empire and the exotic Other swathed in spicy-scented fabrics. Like Victoria, Queen of England and Empress of India, Margaret exists in a liminal state as she is both same and Other, both English and foreign.

But it is the shawls' sensuous quality that truly invades Margaret and transforms her; not only does the smell of the shawls invade the body of the Englishwoman, but their tactile sensation overwhelms her: "She touched the shawls gently as they hung around her, and took a pleasure in their soft feel and their brilliant colours, and rather liked to be dressed in such splendour—enjoying it much as a child would do, with a quiet pleased smile on her lips. Just then the door opened, and Mr. Henry Lennox was suddenly announced. Some of the ladies started back, as if half-ashamed of their feminine interest in dress" (11). Margaret's impulse to touch the fabrics is perhaps sparked by the women's arranging of her: the fabric wants touch, wants sensation, and to best display the fabric, Margaret's body must be touched as well. The ladies' half shame over their "feminine interest" in dress at Mr. Lennox's arrival is not solely dependent on the invasion of a man into their all-female environment; they are not ashamed to be caught being interested in dress, but rather are ashamed to be caught experiencing and enjoying the sensuousness of dress, fabric, and drapery. Mr. Lennox tries to dismiss their frivolous women's concerns by telling Margaret, "I suppose you are all in the depths of business—ladies' business I mean. Very different to my business, which is the real true law business. Playing with shawls is very different work to drawing up settlements" (12). But Margaret defends their "ladies' business": "I knew how you would be amused to find us all so occupied in admiring finery. But really Indian shawls are very perfect things of their kind" (12). This masculine dismissal of fashion as "playing" contrasts sharply with the real work fashion does in this scene. The shawls, while seemingly mere feminine accoutrements, are symbols of wealth, power, prestige, and, above all, England. The "ladies' business" of "playing with shawls" in fact demonstrates and displays the power and wealth of Edith's family to both the reader and to the women for whom Margaret models. When Margaret states that "really Indian shawls are very perfect things of their kind," she is, in fact, correct: they are perfect representations of England's conquests and thus of Englishness itself.

The shawl's symbolic resonance as an object of Englishness furthers its intended purpose as a display of wealth. The duality of the Indian shawl—it is symbolic both of foreign and domestic spaces—only truly comes into consideration when it enters the realm of "ladies' business." Mr. Lennox's lack of understanding, or perhaps his outright refusal to understand, demonstrates how insignificant many nineteenth-century men believed fashionable items were. When Margaret reminds him of the power this fashionable item held when wielded in the hands of middle-class Englishwomen, she offers the understanding that Englishwomen do, indeed, wield power. Margaret's transformation into something altogether new accounts for the fact that the women are only "half-ashamed of their feminine interest in dress." If the Indian shawl had not represented so much, the women would have more reason to feel ashamed of their "playing with shawls."

In *Cranford*, Mrs. Jenkyns is buried in the shawl Peter sends home, even though Miss Matty wonders, "Perhaps it was not reasonable, but what could we do or say?" (58). The "unreasonableness" of burying her mother in the shawl directly concerns the wealth and status that the shawl represents; shawls were often heirlooms, passed from mother to daughter as they are in *North and South*, and perhaps the possession of such expensive fashionable items would have eased Miss Matty's burdens when her finances declined. But for Miss Matty, the memorialization of her mother's virtues as an Englishwoman is more important than her personal financial need. Again, we see the transformative powers of the shawl, which changes Mrs. Jenkyns as it does Margaret; Miss Matty notes that she "looked so lovely" and much younger, and once they "decked her in the long soft folds; she lay, smiling, as if pleased" when "all Cranford came" to see her (58). This shawl, "just such a shawl as she wished for when she was married, and her mother did not give it her" (58), has found what the Cranfordians would understand as its appropriate home at last, eternally on the body of a good Englishwoman, because Englishwomen themselves had transformed its meaning from an article of dress to the representation of English femininity and virtue.

The Altering of France:
Gaskell Creates an Englishness of Dress

The citizens of Cranford, for the most part, stand in opposition to the rapid change and modernization occurring around them. Fashion's mercurial nature and its usual country of origin, France, become suspect to the Amazons. While they cling to their age gone by, their red umbrellas and their gigots, they see Paris as the symbol of the change they cannot abide. The very meaning of Paris is one of change, impulse, and revolution, and therefore is counter to everything Cranford and England believe in. But fashion also changes constantly, as new trends, lines, and ideas take shape, and this ever-changing nature of fashion also becomes inextricably connected with France and its people. France thus represents the best of fashion—the latest styles, the boldest lines—and the worst of fashion—its signal of vanity, its constant change, its costly sway—to Englishwomen such as the Cranford Amazons. What the citizens of Cranford refer to as "that wicked Paris" is characterized by constant change and the belief that the people of France "are always having Revolutions" (39); in contrast, England, encapsulated in the depiction of Cranford, often is seen as characterized by continuity and sameness.

In Cranford, the women script their own fashions according to their own ideals, and more often than not, those ideals align with their understanding of Englishness. Yet some critics feel that fashion can appear to be if not divorced from then at least ignorant of its historical context or its nation of origin, the same as it can be rewritten as both historical and foreign. Hilary M. Schor argues that "The point of dress in Cranford is not to reveal history; fashion is not historical because it has its own history—one of personal history or of individual connections . . . or of the individual meaning within the community but never of the 'wicked' revolutionary traces of, say, France" (100). Schor views Cranford's rewriting of fashion's history as a writing of "personal history" or "individual connections," particularly in a town controlled, populated, and narrated by middle-class women. Thus female authorship in Cranford extends not only to personal history but to personal dress, as well. Yet Cranford's anxieties over the national origin of its fashionable attire to the point of rewriting fashionable origins suggest that while the "*point* of dress in Cranford is not to reveal history" (100, emphasis added), it nevertheless, in fact, does.[13] The assimilation of French fashions into English culture would suggest that England was more influenced by French culture than its citizens would care to believe. Fashion historian Valerie Steele in *Fashion and Eroticism* argues that "A particular new fashion cannot logically be said to 'reflect' developments within English society (such as the movement for women's rights) or particularly English social attitudes, if, in fact, English women copied it from a French model" (6–7). In her article "Reflections on Victorian Fashion Plates," Sharon Marcus similarly reflects on fashion's origins in France, and her argument supports Steele's claims. Marcus remarks, "Despite historiographical claims about the role dress played in creating national identity, British fashion after the Napoleonic wars was transatlantic, and British fashion illustration *was* French. Most French fashion magazines published international coeditions, and the major British fashion magazines had Parisian offices and employed French artists to illustrate Parisian trends" (11). While the origin of most fashions in France does suggest that Victorian England's sense of dress was more facsimile than originality, nineteenth-century Englishwomen not only copied but changed French fashions to suit English sensibilities, or resisted the fashions altogether.[14] Certainly the Englishwomen were responding to the French originals, but ultimately "good" Englishwomen, women successful at embodying and representing Englishness, authored their own texts of fashion by altering and even rejecting specifically French fashions and style.

In *Cranford*, Miss Matty asks Mary Smith to bring her a sea-green turban, quite in style at the time, but Mary Smith resists, claiming that she "had rather that she blamed Drumble and me than disfigured herself with a turban" (82). When Signor Brunoni, an Englishman masquerading as "The Grand Turk, as Miss Pole chose to call him," appears on stage wearing a turban, Miss Matty "turned round, and said to me, in a kind, mild, sorrowful tone:—'You see, my dear, turbans *are* worn'" (87). C. Willett Cunnington's exhaustive study *English Women's Clothing in the*

Nineteenth Century discusses the turban over twenty times throughout the century, tracing its rise and fall and rise again. Several of the descriptions of the turban include foreign adjectives, Arab, Italian, and so on, to bring to mind their countries of origin. Mary Smith refuses Miss Matty's request partly out of fashionable concern—she believes Miss Matty will "disfigure" herself—but also because it just would not do for a woman of Cranford.

In "The Cage at Cranford," an 1863 appendix to her 1853 novel, Elizabeth Gaskell returns both to Cranford town and to the idea of fashion among the Amazons by demonstrating the Cranfordian need to change a French fashion into an English one. This short story introduces the cage, or crinoline, to Cranford, and while she is once again the arbiter of good taste, even worldly Mary Smith cannot understand the significance and purpose of the cage. She writes to Mrs. Gordon, traveling abroad at the time, to bring back a present that is "pretty and new and fashionable" for Miss Pole, as the elderly lady "had just been talking a great deal about Mrs. FitzAdam's caps being so unfashionable" (169). Mary later wishes she had asked for a present that "was not to be too fashionable; for there *is* such a thing" (169, emphasis original) because Mrs. Gordon sends her a cage from Paris, as "they were so much better made in Paris than anywhere else" (170). In these introductory paragraphs, the story fully acknowledges the superiority of France in the world of fashion; it suggests that one should go to Paris for the latest fashions, and one should expect higher quality from the fashions in France than those made anywhere else.

Mary Smith's aside that there "*is* such a thing" as being "too fashionable," however, anticipates the Amazons' argument that fashions, particularly those originating in France, can be absurd. Seemingly no one in Cranford even knows what a cage could be, and the townspeople argue that it is a birdcage (170), a mousetrap (176), or a meat safe (177). When Fanny the maid suggests that it could be a petticoat because "my sister-in-law has got an aunt as lives lady's maid with Sir John's daughter—Miss Arley. And they did say as she wore iron petticoats all made of hoops," the towns-people express their disbelief both that such a thing could exist and that a maid would know of fashions before her employers (176). Even Mary argues against the claim that the "cage" is in fact an undergarment: "such a thing had not been heard of in all Drumble, let alone Cranford, and I was rather looked upon in the light of a fast young woman by all the laundresses of Cranford, because I had two corded petticoats" (176–77).[15] Fanny's recollection of the iron petticoats is due exclusively to her family's position with an aristocratic family; not only does the daughter of Sir

John wears "indecent" undergarments, the servants who dress her and take care of her clothing know about them, too, and freely discuss them with others. The Cranfordians cannot fathom that something as indecent as "a circle of hoops, neatly covered over with calico" (176) could come from anywhere, even France.[16]

"The Cage at Cranford" pokes gentle fun at the crinoline's absurdity; the story's humor is dependent on the crinoline's construction and its novelty, its innovation and French origins. With the aid of the doctor, Mr. Hoggins, himself familiar with the crinoline because of his wife's adoration of Parisian fashions, Mary and Miss Pole discover the cage's actual purpose as a lady's petticoat. The two women are chagrined not because of their lack of knowledge alone but because a man and a maid knew more about fashion than they.[17] Keeping the crinoline seems not to be an option for Miss Pole, and she proposes instead that she and Mary "should cut up the pieces of steel or whalebone—which, to do them justice, were very elastic—and make ourselves two good comfortable English calashes out of them with the aid of a piece of dyed silk which Miss Pole had by her" (179). Miss Pole chooses function over form when she transforms the cage into calashes or folding hoods, and more importantly, she chooses England over France when she makes "good comfortable English calashes" out of a Parisian petticoat.[18] Like Cook, who "was evidently set against the new invention, and muttered about it being all of a piece with French things" (176), Miss Pole disavows the cage's function as anything other than a piece of fashionable nonsense. The transformation of a piece of French fashion into an item of English necessity stretches beyond the idea of modesty and into the realm of function: the calashes are needed in England's rainy climate.[19] Further, the shift from an item intended to accentuate a woman's lower body to an item intended to protect a woman's head also argues for the Cranfordians' subtle defiance in changing a French exposure of a woman's body to an English protection of it.

Yet the fact remains that the majority of fashions worn and purchased in nineteenth-century England originate in France either in manufacture or style, even those fashions enjoyed in Cranford, where everyone knows each other. When critics question the possibility of a true English fashion at this time, they suggest that national fashion only can occur if those fashions are original to the nation in question.[20] This interpretation divorces items of fashion from the bodies that wear them and discounts the sheer fact that women accessorized, altered, or even transformed their clothing multiple times, for multiple trends, exhibiting multiple styles.[21]

To view these fashions as solely French, then, is to disregard an essential part of women's participation in fashion history. The point of fashion in *Cranford* may seem to be modesty but it is also change; while fashions may be mercurial in France, they are also ever-changing in England. The essence of English style, as we can see through the women of Cranford, is alteration.

Thus there is an "English fashion" in Cranford, and it is a conscious rejection of what is considered fashionable in Paris as well as in London. Because she understands London, Mary Smith helps us recognize Gaskell's gently mocking tone of both fashionable imperatives and fashionable rejections. In making an article of clothing more suited for their needs, the townspeople of Cranford create English fashion, here defined by its popularity, its usefulness, its modesty, and, most importantly, its rejection of the common assumptions of fashionability. While "The Cage at Cranford" gives us a humorous view of the crinoline's migration from France to England, it signals Gaskell's deeper understanding of national anxieties evident in mid-nineteenth-century England. Her presentation of these anxieties, encapsulated in the seemingly trivial world of fashion, demonstrates that women *were* engaged with nation, even women as disconnected as those from Cranford.

In her 1895 work *The Gentlewoman's Book of Dress*, Fanny Douglas argues that "Good dressing, like charity, should begin at home" (43), which is a sentiment that reflects a vast majority of Englishwomen's attitudes toward dress throughout the nineteenth century. Cranford's Amazons also believe that good fashions begin at home; their disdain of France and concern over the influence that nation, and in particular, "that wicked Paris," holds over England, greatly influence their consumer choices. The fashions from the world beyond must be either assimilated or appropriated—a shawl from India represents England's imperial power—or disguised or obliterated—a crinoline from France represents England's constant national threat. The Cranfordian Amazons form a community with their red umbrellas, their turbans, and their good material; their domestic agendas—the home scenes that are microcosmic examples of larger domestic concerns—fulfill Ellis's call for the women of England to protect its symbolic borders. Ellis justifies her conduct tract and its purpose by arguing that her work intends "to show how intimate is the connexion which exists between the **women** of England, and the **moral** character maintained by their country in the scale of nations" (38, emphasis original) and that Englishwomen "preside" over the domestic sphere

(39). What Ellis argues, and what Cranford's Amazons prove, is that these "minor morals of domestic life" are as important as imperial conquests and expansions to the creation and maintenance of England's cultural character. The crisis of national authenticity is represented in *Cranford* by small-scale French invasions and in England by very real concerns over the introduction of foreign characteristics into the very character of England. As the definition of "Englishness" changes with the face of the nation, so, too, do the expectations for "women's duty" and the figuring of authentic Englishwomen as protectors as well as symbols of cultural legitimacy.

Chapter Two

William Thackeray's Fashionable Humbugs and Unfashionable Darlings

Consuming National Distinctions of Dress

Figure 2.1. Roxey Ann Caplin's Corset 1851, displayed at the Great Exhibition. *Source:* Courtesy of the London Museum. Used with permission.

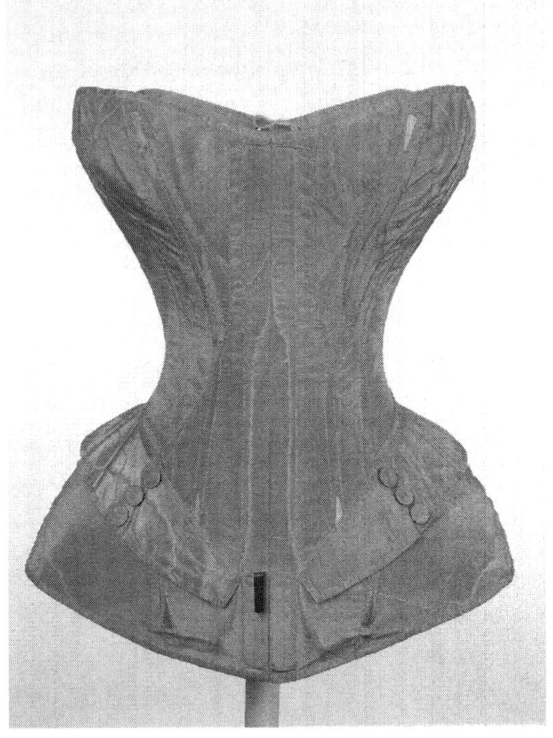

There are two Roxey Ann Caplin corsets in the archives of the London Museum: a blue one and a green one, both made in 1851 and both displayed at the Great Exhibition. Caplin was concerned with the dress reform movement and, in particular, reforming corsets to make them more comfortable and easier to wear for the women who purchased them.[1]

The details now seem onerous to a time when we do not wear corsets, but at the time, they were quite revolutionary. The busk is a split busk, so that there is distribution of the stiffness in the front. There is a high back to help with posture. A hook on the front of the corset helps hold up petticoats, and the buttons on the hips also have skirt-carrying purposes.[2] The color is what always fascinates me. Such a beautiful green-blue satin, meant for display, in the way that red crinoline is meant for display. And according to the London Museum description, it was only meant for a display. The description notes, "Nothing but white, grey or black corsets being made for the respectable public," which makes one wonder: Why make it such a satiny green in the first place? Would a woman see this corset and desire its unusual color? But for whom would she wear it? And why? Who sees the corset when it is on a body instead of on display? A lover, another woman, servants, and, of course, the wearer. In the same way that women now buy beautiful lingerie to wear for themselves, women then also bought beautiful things to wear close to the body. Perhaps the wearer would feel more confident in her green silk corset or her red crinoline. Or perhaps she didn't. Perhaps it didn't fit her right or carry with it the same tiny waist other corsets gave. Perhaps her friends tittered behind their hands at her looser self, like Becky Sharp does to Amelia Sedley in William Thackeray's *Vanity Fair*.[3]

Half-French and a conniving social fraud, William Thackeray's scandalous "love to hate her and hate to love her" character Becky Sharp is not socially acceptable to the middle- and upper-class persons with whom she spends so much time in the novel.[4] She is, however, quite capable of constructing a charming identity because she affects the desirable characteristics of a fashionable woman as well as a Frenchwoman among the English. "Honest old Dobbin" may see through Becky's disguise and recognize "What a humbug that woman is!" but George Osborne, Amelia Sedley's husband and would-be lover of Becky, dismisses the concept of "Humbug—acting!" in Becky's character, because he refuses to see through her pretense to the evident artificiality she displays (Thackeray 338). Rather, like Amelia who becomes "overpowered by the flash and dazzle and the fashionable talk of her worldly rival" (338), George is blinded by Becky's constructed self. Her penchant for acting and her desire for fashion and worldliness mark her as a "humbug"; her clothes and her sparkle mark her as a savvy consumer. It seems that Becky is all "flash and dazzle" and no real substance.

Amelia Sedley acts as Becky's foil in Thackeray's novel, and I use the word "act" in two ways: Thackeray scripts her character as a counterpoint to Becky's, and Amelia herself willingly and actively performs as Becky's opposite. The shy innocent to Becky's flamboyant coquette, the unfashionable Englishwoman to Becky's fashionable French, Amelia succeeds as the ideal woman England proclaims it desires because she looks and behaves "naturally." The first descriptions of Amelia concern her "guileless and good-natured" self, her face that "blushed with rosy health, and her lips with the freshest of smiles," and her eyes "which sparkled with the brightest and honestest good-humour" (43). Like Becky, Amelia sparkles, which *seems* to be a gift of nature rather than fashionable artifice. And Amelia's nature is, of course, bestowed upon her by two middle-class English parents and not, as Becky's is, by an English artist and a French opera girl. However, this naturalness is just as conscious as Becky's fashioning, marking both women as humbugs.

William Thackeray's *Vanity Fair* offers a dichotomous presentation of French and English women[5] that is rooted in the consumption of fashion and of nation. Through its comparison of Becky Sharp Crawley and Amelia Sedley Osborne, Thackeray's novel exposes England's suspicions of women's conscious style and fashionable consumption. As style is associated with artificiality, purposeful and mindful consumerism, and—particularly in nineteenth-century England—France, it functions as a signal of deception and deceit to the English. Therefore, Englishwomen's supposed ignorance of dress—yet continuous, seemingly accidental, beauty and style—would signal that their "natural" style is rooted in the innocence and purity of their consequence of birth and not in their learned consumption and artificial construction of a fashionable self. What seems to be the unconscious self-stylizing of Amelia is in fact clumsy, feigned ignorance of fashionable dress and personal beauty; this feigned ignorance is presented in the novel as equivalent to Becky's carefully constructed and willfully gained knowledge of the same, marking them both as fashionable humbugs. When Thackeray presents both Becky Sharp and Amelia Sedley as artificially constructed, he argues that their fashion and style are the results of learned behaviors and careful articulation of artifice and manner and not, as so many would argue, the result of arbitrary national distinctions.

"Natural" Beauty and "Artificial" Style:
English and French Humbugs

Becky Sharp is a dangerous woman in Thackeray's novel because, despite her nation of origin and her low station of birth, she moves within the middle and upper classes with ease and comfort; through Rawdon Crawley, she marries into the aristocracy; she solicits sexual advances and marriage proposals from several high-ranking members of English aristocracy; she receives costly gifts from Englishmen that the narrator slyly suggests if they actually "went to gentlemen's lawful wives and daughters, what a profusion of jewellery there would be exhibited in the genteelest homes of Vanity Fair!" (352); most importantly, she conceives a child of mixed, English and French, blood. Throughout Thackeray's novel, both the characters and the narrator emphasize Becky's artificiality again and again, and this excessive repetition underscores the nineteenth-century panic over a woman's artificiality and its signals of foreignness. Becky invents her own ancestors (48). She is "artful" (67), a "humbug" (338), and an actress (491) with "a habit of play-acting and fancy dressing" (612). While these accusations seem in step with a novel that proclaims itself "without a hero," the same accusations from literary critics seem almost extreme. She is painted as "an unscrupulous and greedy representative of the rising middle classes" (Zlotnick 57), the promoter of "female chicanery" (Jadwin 666), a "sirenlike heroine" (Dyer 197), and, most importantly for this study, "an artist" (Sheets 421). Robin Ann Sheets furthers the discussion of Becky's artifice and her artfulness by arguing that not only does Thackeray write Becky Sharp as an artist, but Thackeray writes an entire novel about art (420), its deceit (421), and its potential for counterfeit (422) as well. Becky's designation as an "artist" calls forth her capacity for artful deceit, her construction of her family, her self, and her feelings, which are all part, as Sheets reminds us, of Becky's capacity for mimesis; the novel demonstrates, again and again, Becky's imitative skills and powers of performance (421).

As Becky's English foil, Amelia is presented as a demure, charmingly clumsy girl with seemingly so little idea of her own style and beauty that she cannot help but fail at constructing herself. Seen as a "natural" beauty, Amelia and her actions often are described with the terms "natural" (70), "artless" (148), or "unaffected" (148). Even contemporary literary critics fall under the sway of Amelia's gentle awkwardness and see it as the consequence of nature, rather than a combination of nature, nation, and, most importantly for this study, learned skills through a careful and thorough education. Judith Fisher, for example, argues that "Amelia's appearance is the consequence of her own nature" in that her eyes, skin, lips, and good humor create a physique as well as a personality (400). For Fisher, Amelia's appearance is directly correlated not only with the features with which she was born but also with her "good humor" and "own nature." Robin Ann Sheets reminds us that "As often as Becky is called artful, Amelia is called artless; the word refers to both her innocence and her ineptitude" (423) as Thackeray's novel presents her. Amelia's innocence often is revealed in her downcast eyes or her blushing face; her ineptitude, however, speaks to an ignorance that does not seem learned, when, in fact, it is.

This fashionable failure can be read as a "natural" mistake by a Victorian audience; it takes place because Amelia, as an Englishwoman, supposedly cannot construct artificiality. In the world Thackeray creates, as well as the world in which he writes, artfulness is contrasted with artlessness, as France is contrasted with England and as Becky's theoretical artifice is contrasted with Amelia's theoretical naturalness.[6] These contrasts demonstrate the similarities rather than the differences between England's assumptions about its women and the women of other nations. Kit Dobson argues that Amelia Sedley is just as guilty of performance as Becky Sharp is and that the constant repetition of the word "natural" to describe Amelia is in fact a performance of the expectations of English femininity.[7] Both the constant repetition of the words "art," "artless," and "artifice" in Thackeray's novel as well as the novel's sly acknowledgment of its interest in performance through its introduction of the stage of Vanity Fair itself expose Thackeray's awareness and purposeful scripting of his characters' performances. From small-scale stagings of friendship, familial expectation, and domestic duties to larger, subtle scriptings of nineteenth-century ideologies of, and expectations for, domesticity, nationality, class, and gender expectations, Thackeray's characters understand the value of a good performance. My interest here, however, is not solely in feminine performance—whether conscious or not—but in fashionability and style; through artifice, affectation, and those minute details of manner and of dress, Becky and Amelia possess individual styles that are, in the end, nationally ascribed.

As Thackeray's characters try to sort out what is "natural" and what is "artificial," they use the same method as their nineteenth-century reading audience: an examination of a woman's style, that individualized and socialized collection of fashion, manners, and deportment. Therefore, these presentations are rooted not only in the national but also in the fashionable, two realms that are, as we see consistently in nineteenth-century texts, intrinsically connected. For Victorian England, this was divided according to nationalist lines, and fashion critics have paid particular attention to the national distinctions the nineteenth century made between English and French women. Valerie Steele's influential fashion study *Fashion and Eroticism: Ideals of Feminine Beauty from the Victorian Era to the Jazz Age* notes that while the English continued to insist on "natural" beauty, "the French, on the other hand, often implied that natural beauty was only the beginning. A woman learned to *become* beautiful" (135, emphasis original). The assumption in England, ultimately, was that "learning to become beautiful" was an unattractive and suspicious trait in women.

These beliefs are not without historical precedent; throughout the nineteenth century, fashion and manners texts separated English and French women's approaches to dress and beauty, creating the distinction between nature and construction, between natural and artificial, as the distinction between England and France. In an 1861 text about life in Paris, the pseudonymous Chroniqueuse finds "how plain, alongside of these [Frenchwomen], appear English girls, who, with ten times more natural beauty, seem so ugly with their poke bonnets, ugly and coarse stuff gowns that cling to the figure, while the little short jackets add to the uncouthness of the *tout ensemble!* 'As badly dressed as an *Anglaise*,' has got to be a proverb among the Parisians; and surely they are right" (157). To Chroniqueuse, English girls appear "plain" alongside their fashionable French sisters, despite possessing "ten times more natural beauty." To an English reading public, however, these girls are triumphant in their appearance abroad, as their beauty is not diminished or overshadowed by the flounces and petticoats, the artful construction that fashion—particularly French fashion—demands.

In her 1878 treatise on fashion, aestheticism, and appearance, *The Art of Beauty*, Mrs. H. R. Haweis (Mary Eliza Haweis) encompasses the prevailing Victorian attitude toward the history of dress and popular fashion trends and instructs her readers on how to choose the most becoming dress and ornamentation. While she strives to instruct all women on proper color coordination and on draping fabrics according to natural bodylines, she cannot avoid calling attention to Englishwomen's superiority in the world of beauty. As Haweis argues, "The Englishwomen are considered by all nations to be among the most beautiful in the world, whilst the French are commonly far less gifted by nature, but a Frenchwoman understands how to hide her defects and enhance her beauties to a far greater extent than an Englishwoman—and this, not because her moral character is necessarily lower, but simply because she belongs to an artistic race, cultivating aesthetic tastes" (258–59). Haweis presents her belief in the superiority of Englishwomen's beauty as a consequence of nature and birth. Frenchwomen, in contrast, excel in the artificial construction of beauty; their "artistic race" understands "how to hide [their] defects and enhance [their] beauties," traits Englishwomen, it seems, are not capable of. In Haweis's estimation, this is "not because [a Frenchwoman's] moral character is necessarily lower" than an Englishwoman's, but the adverb "necessarily," suggests that a lowered moral character may at least be partly responsible. By establishing a division between women's artificiality and naturalness, between standards for constructed beauty and natural beauty, Haweis reiterates Victorian England's common division between French and English. Haweis's and Chroniqueuse's texts, later in the century than Thackeray's novel, still exhibit the prevailing understandings of nationality evident in the Victorian mindset. Therefore, with the addition of Thackeray's text, we see that from the 1840s to the 1870s, England still believes in the national distinctions between it and France.

French Habits of Playacting and Fancy Dress: Thackeray's Fashionable Humbug

Victorian England wanted to believe that Englishwomen were, unlike Becky Sharp, incapable of constructing a fashionable self, but as Thackeray's novel reveals, this was an unfulfilled and unrealistic desire. Characters' fashionability must be examined in conjunction with an exploration of nineteenth-century England's understanding of national distinctions in dress. Such an examination allows an exploration of Thackeray's novel that highlights the double-bind in Victorian England regarding fashionable women's clothing: to be fashionable, one must be aware of the fashions and the ideas they convey, but to be a good Englishwoman, one must pretend to be ignorant of the artificiality of fashion and persuade others of one's ignorance. When viewed with a Victorian understanding of fashion and national identification, it seems only logical that Becky Sharp, half-French herself, would be obsessed with fashion. Thackeray's novel seems overly concerned with fashion as it details Becky's clothing again and again, particularly in discussions of Becky's stage acting and tableau constructing and always in conjunction with her social climbing. Becky's concerns with fashion are the concerns of an ambitious woman, as she manipulates fashion and the common understanding and interpretation of fashion to climb the social ladder. Becky Sharp is constructed as a dangerous woman throughout the novel because she knowingly constructs herself; she is aware of the artificial nature of fashion.[8] As Ellen Bayuk Rosenman notes, in the nineteenth century, fashion was deemed dangerous because it was both artistic and sexually aware (15); a woman's sophistication and self-construction in the arena of fashion speak of secret initiations and rites. Not only does Becky understand this, she also revels in it. She stages tableaux in which she is the star, the figure to be admired and fawned over by her male admirers, and her clothing speaks to these desires: she is admired and fawned over because she dresses to be so. Sharon Marcus in "Reflections on Victorian Fashion Plates" argues that "those who sell fashion, like those who produce dolls, create simulacra of femininity not for men but for *women and girls* to scrutinize, handle, and consume. To market femininity to women is to use hyperfeminine objects to solicit a female gaze and to incite female fantasy" (4, emphasis original). Marcus argues that the looking and looking back of feminine fashion is not grounded in heteroeroticism but rather in homoeroticism; thus, fashion is worn by women for the visual pleasure of other women.

This certainly holds true in Thackeray's novel, but this argument can be taken even further. The solicitation of the female gaze of which Marcus speaks is less the issue in *Vanity Fair* than the power of women to "scrutinize, handle, and consume." I believe that the marketing of femininity is not where the power of fashion lies in *Vanity Fair* but, rather, with women's consumption and the reading of fashion. Fashion is, I argue, an arena to which Victorian women are relegated because it is seen as trivial. Becky's interest in dress and, most importantly, her use of dress prove this belief to be false; fashion is not a trivial realm, because it can be used to promote personal agendas, convey or assume national affiliation, or, in Becky's case, move within national class ranks. To counter this, the Victorian audience dismisses fashionable know-how as simple foreign deception; true Englishwomen would not have such arcane and dangerous knowledge. Thackeray uses Becky and England's distaste for her to highlight the hypocrisy evident in these fears.

Because fashionable women like Becky Sharp understand the artificiality of dress and the presentation of self that it allows, they are familiar with both the consumption and interpretation of fashion. With their seemingly innate knowledge of fashion, women such as Becky are privy to skills heretofore usually associated with men: reading, interpreting, and consuming objects and, most importantly, women. Becky possesses, therefore, a small piece of masculine power; it is no wonder that she is usually in the company of men in the novel, for this reason, if not for her sexual misadventures. What Becky Sharp best demonstrates and what Thackeray's novel best implies is that women's fashion and, through it, constructions of self, are not dangerous only because they solicit the male or the female gaze; fashion is dangerous also because it is made to solicit any gaze at all.

To complicate the groundwork laid by previous critics, particularly Sheets and Marcus, I believe we can take Becky's power of performance and conscious, purposeful consumption of fashion one step further to examine how her artistry, her artfulness, her performance, and her mimicry are all parts of herself that Becky *enjoys*. Ultimately, what is dangerous about Becky is that she is believed to have mastered feminine secrets and has learned to enjoy her body through her hyperstylizing. Because she is half-French, Becky has awareness of the seemingly mystical fashion knowledge supposedly unavailable to Englishwomen. But further, Becky Sharp is artificial because she chooses to be so; the reader never sees any sign that there is a real Becky beneath the façade of the performer, the flirtatious lover, the good wife, the social climber, the capricious friend, and the dozens of other roles that Becky plays throughout the novel. Like all good performances, these roles depend heavily on costume change to carry the weight of staged authenticity; or, as Patricia Marks reminds us, "Becky is nothing without her finery" (82).

Once she establishes a modicum of respectability as the wife of Rawdon Crawley, Becky no longer receives her dresses, shawls, and accoutrements of fashion secondhand; her constructed self, therefore, is no longer a borrowed self.[9] She is completely aware of every ring or bracelet, of every fold or bow, and even her surroundings would never dare to clash with Becky's *ensemble*. While seated with "a party of gentlemen around her" (444), Becky is observed in the candlelight by Lord Steyne:

[The candles] lighted up Rebecca's figure to admiration, as she sate [*sic*] on a sofa covered with a pattern of gaudy flowers. She was in a pink dress, that looked as fresh as a rose; her dazzling white arms and shoulders were half-covered with a thin hazy scarf through which they sparkled; her hair hung in

> curls round her neck; one of her little feet peeped out from the
> fresh crisp folds of the silk: the prettiest little foot in the pret-
> tiest little sandal in the finest silk stocking in the world. (445)

Becky sits on a floral-patterned sofa to match her pink dress that looked, fittingly, "fresh as a rose." The sofa and Becky match entirely too well, just as the candlelight hits her a bit too perfectly. But it is not just for the "ice and coffee . . . , the best in London" that "the men came to her house to finish the night" (444); men like Lord Steyne come because Becky has displayed herself to utmost perfection. While the "candles lighted up Lord Steyne's shining bald head" and his "twinkling bloodshot eyes, surrounded by a thousand wrinkles," demonstrating every physical fault of the aristocrat, those same candles light instead Becky's "figure to admiration" (445). In her own things and in her own home, Becky is able to fashion a self to her best advantage. By matching her clothing to her surroundings, by best situating herself in the candlelight, and by surrounding herself only with admirers, Becky ensures her social success among a small but elite crowd, a success dependent on her knowledge of fashion and her ability to display her best features.[10] The national danger here stems from the fact that not only has Becky inserted herself into the English aristocracy by marriage, and the middle class by friendship, she also has gained the admiration and attention of several Englishmen precisely *because* she has constructed a beautiful and pleasing self.

Thackeray's novel satirizes the differences between Englishwomen's and Frenchwomen's approaches to fashion in one particular scene, the confrontation of Becky Sharp Crawley and Amelia Sedley Osborne at the infamous June 15, 1815, Brussels ball the night before the company is called off to war. This ball has been discussed greatly in criticism and history for its impact on the soldiers and its proximity to warfare, but like Thackeray's narrator's, our place is with the noncombatants (346). For Becky Sharp, the ball represents the best of such shining moments for her; her utter grasp of fashion, of self-construction through clothing, and of those stylish secrets to which she and not Amelia is privy allow her to construct a self that is, without a doubt, the belle of the ball. The narrator tells us that while Amelia's "appearance was an utter failure," Becky Sharp's "*debut* was, on the contrary, very brilliant. She arrived very late. Her face was radiant; her dress perfection" (342). She is swarmed by men and gossiped about by women, who "agreed that her manners were fine, her air *distingué*" (342), two points that Becky proves complete falsities when she walks over to Amelia and "finish[es] the poor child at once" (342). Becky's shining moment is dependent not on the clothes that she is wearing, but rather on her reading and consumption of the clothes other women are wearing.[11] She reads Amelia's dress as an artificial covering of awkwardness and discomfort: "Mrs. Rawdon ran and greeted affectionately her dearest Amelia, and began forthwith to patronize her. She found fault with her friend's dress, and her hairdresser, and wondered how she could be so *chaussée*, and vowed that she must send her *corsetière* the next morning" (342). And as if this long reprimand was not enough, Becky then "left her bouquet and shawl by Amelia's side, and tripped off with George to dance" (343). When Becky reads Amelia's ball dress, she reads not only Amelia's inability to wear fashionable clothing but also her inability to dress herself in appropriate and flattering dress. She sees through Amelia's façade to her corset; by offering to send her *corsetière*, Becky takes her reading even further to state that it is Amelia and not her clothing that is a cause for fashionable crisis.

I quote this passage at length because this scene functions as the crux of the nineteenth-century fashionable argument highlighted in Thackeray's novel: there is a distinct difference between Englishwomen and Frenchwomen that is seemingly recognizable through not only what they wear but how well they wear it. At this moment, Becky's utter artificiality and Amelia's utter naïveté at disguising artificiality are nowhere better seen. Becky's knowledge of fashion and power in the fashionable world allow her perfect dress and radiant face; indeed, her fashionable knowledge lends itself perfectly to her evaluation of Amelia. In a discussion of snobbery and consumerism in *Vanity Fair*, Joseph Litvak argues that "in a marketplace mobbed with cool customers, the successful consumer must be able conspicuously to consume not just commodities but other consumers; or—to put it more tastefully—she must consume the *consumption* of other consumers" (63, emphasis original). Becky is, above all else, a successful consumer. Her power lies in artificiality and in recognition, in that secret French knowledge of dress that she possesses, and in her subversive ability to read, consume, and interpret.[12] At the Brussels ball, Becky not only reads but consumes, and as Litvak reminds us, she not only consumes but consumes consumption; in addition to being a siren and a humbug, Becky becomes, in this moment, a succubus, feeding on fashion faux pas. She is able to suck the life and shine out of Amelia's evening, and all because "Women only know how to wound so" (Thackeray 343). She understands that Amelia is just as artificially constructed as she is. The irony of this moment is that Amelia, an Englishwoman, is constructed poorly.[13]

Further, Becky's knowledge of women, of bodies, and even of fashion allows her to recognize that Amelia's failure is not due to her fashionable tastes, but rather her husband's. It is George and not Amelia who has "commanded new dresses and ornaments of all sorts" for Mrs. Osborne for the ball (341), and it is George who feels "with a sort of rage" Amelia's appearance as "an utter failure" (342). George believes that "he had behaved very handsomely in getting her new clothes" (342), but in fact, the clothes he has acquired for his wife lead to her ridicule and scorn at the hands of Becky Sharp. George's responsibility extends even to Amelia's body itself; her corset and dress fit so poorly because Amelia is, at this point in the novel, pregnant with George's child.[14] Becky sees Amelia's clothing as a façade. By calling attention to Amelia's poorly worn corset, Becky calls attention to Amelia's figure, the actual body beneath the clothed body on display for the attendees of the ball. That figure is not disguised by the corset Amelia wears; Amelia is visibly pregnant, in public, at a ball.[15] Becky understands that the female body, particularly the pregnant body, should be shaped and disguised by the corset. She recognizes Amelia's unfashionable presentation as the artificial presentation it is: a poor attempt to ape fashionable dress—acquired by her husband—and a poor attempt to disguise the growing pregnant body—also, in truth, George's fault. What we see in the character foils of Becky Sharp and Amelia Sedley is a nationalistic double standard; the Englishwoman and her knowledge of fashion and style cannot be proclaimed to be artificial, as to do so would be to acknowledge Englishwomen's understanding of the artificiality of style. Yet "natural" beauty and style do not exist, as Amelia's poor attempt to disguise her pregnant body presents. By its very construction, "naturalness" is learned, and therefore there is no such standard as "natural" style; all that remains is artificial, stylized, and learned naturalness.

English Manners and Natural Timidity: Thackeray's Darling

Only seven years after the publication of *Vanity Fair*, Frederick Audax's *A Hint from Modesty to the Ladies of England on the Fashion of Low-Dressing* urges Englishwomen not to be swayed by the lure of fashion and its many artifices. He argues that artifices are "unworthy" of the women of England (iv), particularly because, "An English woman! Who can tell her praise? Who can even most faintly trace all her excellencies? To say that she is a pattern to every country blessed with civilization, is to say nothing that is not in course. . . . And how beautiful! All fair and all lovely she is! In her the North and the South meet, drop every blemish, and unite their beauties in a model of Nature!" (7) Audax claims that Englishwomen are "a pattern to every country blessed with civilization" and that their domesticity, generosity, and modesty (7) are unparalleled. But Audax also takes his praise beyond his countrywomen's superior inner qualities to call attention to their outer beauty. In Audax's opinion, the Englishwoman is the result of the unification of "the North and South" into a "model of Nature." For the author, Englishwomen's beauty is dependent on the beauty of Nature; he calls attention to geographical regions to claim that Englishwomen's beauty is formed by the melding of two such regions' ideals. They have no need for artifice and fashion to make their outward appearance appealing, as Nature has already been so generous.

Yet Amelia Sedley, representative of all of these good English qualities, is a social failure, and Becky Sharp, reviled so often for her artificiality and written as the antithesis of the good Englishwoman Audax and others claim to desire, is a social success. Thackeray portrays Becky as accomplished in everything her society claims desirable for their women yet still dismisses her as false and artificial; Amelia, however, is portrayed as natural and unconscious of how to construct a fashionable self but fails again and again. Becky Sharp fulfills every obligation regarding the art of conversation, beauty, and dress set forth by fashion tracts and manners texts such as Sarah Stickney Ellis's *The Women of England* or Mary Eliza Haweis's *The Art of Beauty*, yet despite it all, the text marks her as foreign, as a "humbug," and as artificial.[16] Ellis tells her readers that "Women have the choice of many means of bringing their principles into exercise, and of obtaining influence, both in their own domestic sphere, and in society at large. Amongst the most important of these is **conversation**" (119, emphasis original), a charge with which Becky Sharp most happily complies. Miss Crawley, Rebecca's benefactor and champion prior to her marriage to Rawdon, declares "little Miss Sharp" to be "the only person fit to talk to in the country!" (141). Most of Becky's charm comes from her penchant for mimicry, and Miss Crawley "laughed heartily at a perfect imitation of Miss Briggs and her grief, which Rebecca described to her" (171). But even Becky Sharp's acting and conversational skills cannot withstand the onslaught of Amelia Sedley, "who came forward so timidly and so gracefully" with a "sweet blushing face" to meet Miss Crawley that the elderly lady declares her "charming" and spoke of her "with rapture half-a-dozen times that day" (178). It is not Amelia's conversational skills or playacting that infatuates Miss Crawley, but rather the grand lady's "good taste. She liked natural manners—a little timidity only set them off" (178). For Miss Crawley, Amelia's appeal lies in her "natural manners" and "timidity," two traits that, it would seem, are inherent. Yet as the existence of so many conduct and fashion tracts attest, manners and style are learned; it is important, therefore, for a woman to learn to appear *unaware* of this knowledge.

For both women, the argument that pits artifice against naturalness is wholly dependent on recognition by the English reading—and viewing—public. The novel's presentation of Englishwoman Amelia Sedley and half-Frenchwoman Becky Sharp relies heavily on national stereotypes with particular regard to fashion. Becky's artificiality, demonstrated by her existence on credit, her hand-me-down clothes, and her humbuggery, stands in sharp contrast to Amelia's "natural" manners, seeming naïveté, and supposed unawareness of fashion. Becky's constant successes in the fashionable world are the result of the approval and admiration of men and foreign women rather than of the social arbiters: middle-class Englishwomen. When she and Rawdon go to Paris, the narrator notes that "Her success in Paris was remarkable. All the French ladies voted her charming. She spoke their language admirably. She *adopted at once* their grace, their liveliness, their manner" (412, emphasis added). Becky's fashionability relies not only on her talent for mimicry and art but also on her adaptability. In England, and among the Englishwomen in Brussels, Becky imitates their fashions and manners; among the French, Becky does the same. It is important to note here that Becky does not fall back on a supposedly natural racial instinct for French grace, liveliness, or manner, as writers like Mary Eliza Haweis might argue that Frenchwomen inherently have. Rather, she adopts her current society's manners and customs, and for this is considered "the gayest and most admired of Englishwomen" (413). Becky's talent for reading and consuming fashion, when coupled with her mastery of staging, allows her to mimic the women of her acquaintance. In this sense, she reads the society around her not only for what its citizens are but also for what they expect their outsiders to be. As a result, in England, Becky is most assuredly French, while in France, she is most assuredly English. The fact that she can claim no country as her own in a social setting lends itself to her cosmopolitanism and reinforces the image of Becky as "a most artful and dangerous person" (413). She understands how to construct a personal and a national self, but she does it too well in England; Becky is free of any of the awkward gestures and innocence that Amelia supposedly possesses. This perfection of presentation, a self too put together, is what ultimately marks Becky as French.

Amelia, in contrast, is "the best, the kindest, the gentlest, the sweetest girl in England" according to George Osborne (253), and while this praise is exaggerated, it is important in its qualifications. In England, Amelia is indeed ranked among the kindest and gentlest of girls, because in England, Amelia is valued and praised for her submissiveness and demureness. But as we see at the beginning of *Vanity Fair*, all of these traits—style, deportment, manners, and carriage—can be learned as well as inherited. Amelia's first introduction in the novel is not through appearance but rather through her headmistress's letter to her parents: "Those virtues which characterise the young English gentlewoman, those accomplishments which become her birth and station, will not be found wanting in the amiable Miss Sedley, whose *industry* and *obedience* have endeared her to her instructors, and whose delightful sweetness of temper has charmed her *aged* and her *youthful* companions" (40, emphasis original). The English virtues for which Amelia is most praised are her industry and obedience, and her temper and amiability have made her a favorite among the school, but her "*deportment and carriage, so requisite for every young lady of fashion*" are found in need of work (40, emphasis original). While Amelia's "industry and obedience"—two personal aspects of her character—are praised, her fashionability and presentation of self are found wanting. Miss Pinkerton gives instructions on how to solve this deficit in Amelia's character—use of the backboard for "four hours daily during the next three years" (40)—but never once does she suggest that Amelia cannot *learn* to acquire "that dignified *deportment and carriage*." What Miss Pinkerton's letter suggests instead is that such signifiers of fashionable awareness are, in fact, learned, and not inherited; Miss Pinkerton acknowledges the artificiality of fashionable women.

Amelia is just as affected as Becky, or as any other woman in the novel, despite the veneer of naturalness she possesses. Mrs. O'Dowd declares that Amelia, "a natural and unaffected person, had none of that artificial shamefacedness which her husband mistook for delicacy on his own part" (327), although, in truth, she does. Amelia's presentations of innocence appear more natural but are in fact just as artificial. When her family teases her about George Osborne, Amelia, "hanging down her head, blushed as only young ladies of seventeen know how to blush" (67). This posturing presents Amelia as modest and humble, but it, too, is a learned response of modesty and humility. Even her blush, labeled as secretive knowledge only available to "young ladies of seventeen," appears as a triggered response to the mention of her young gentleman; "young ladies of seventeen," on the marriage market and aware of the effect of their appearances on the male public, would understand the effect of those blushes, as well. Mary Ann O'Farrell reminds us that nineteenth-century novels and their novelists use the blush as a means of articulation, and that "by means of its attentions to blushing as a perceived event of the body, the [nineteenth-century English] novel suggests that—in seeming involuntarily and reliably to betray a deep self—blushing assists at the conversion of legibility into a sense of identity and centrality," ultimately becoming in this sense "an act of self-expression" (5). Seen as involuntary, the blush is a way of making the private aspects of the body public; the blush is blood rushing to the skin, a response to shock, horror, excitement, shame, and other internal markers of personal revelation. But the blush is also about knowledge; O'Farrell argues that "innocence, after all, is compromised by the knowledge that raises the blush" (18). Amelia, in the end, despite the novel's insistence on her guilelessness, *knows how to blush*. Her understanding of an Englishwoman's middle-class feminine style is a learned response to behaviors, and through the presentation of her clumsy, awkward fashioning and pretty blushes, Amelia scripts the very artificiality Victorian England claims to despise—and it loves her, as an Englishwoman, for it.

The "artificial shamefacedness" that is not as evident in Amelia is very much evident in Becky Sharp. At Becky's first dinner with the Sedleys, Becky's innocence is dependent on "holding her green eyes downwards" on her white gown and on her "bare shoulders as white as snow," all creating "the picture of youth, unprotected innocence, and humble virgin simplicity," implying that Becky is "very modest" (60). Becky's "picture of youth" is in truth a picture; it is a projection constructed by Becky's artfulness and her ability to best portray the attributes her audience desires. She understands that a successful and advantageous marriage with the laughable but wealthy Jos Sedley would lead to her social success, and Becky instructs herself to maintain the façade of innocence and attentiveness, as a blushing virgin would do: " 'I must be very quiet,' thought Rebecca, 'and very much interested about India' " (60). In contrast, Amelia Sedley enjoys some fashionable success once more when Dobbin returns from

India. The men in his company, "as usual, liked her artless kindness and simple refined demeanour" (698). While the men "as usual" appreciate Amelia's artlessness and simplicity, they are reiterating their desire for the traits England so desires in its women: the appearance of artlessness and the presentation of naturalness.

Amelia appears as the celebrated Englishwoman because she exists "in contrast"; that is, we see who Amelia is through seeing who she decidedly is not. Her "artless kindness and simple refined demeanour" stand ever in contrast to Becky's artfulness and ostentatiousness. On the honeymoon tour, Amelia "joins *her* regiment" and in truth she possesses George's company with "her simple, artless behavior, and modest kindness of demeanour" (316, emphasis added). When "it became the fashion, indeed, among all the honest young fellows of the –th [*sic*], to adore and admire Mrs. Osborne," (316) Amelia finds herself with "a little triumph, which flushed her spirits and made her eyes sparkle" (321). This triumph that flushes Amelia's spirits flushes her face, as well; her social successes bring a healthy blush to her cheeks and shine to her eyes. Unencumbered by the fashionable "flash and substance" that Becky Sharp might wear, Amelia's physical presentation would appear, as some nineteenth-century writers would suggest, "plain," but her careful construction of fashion and dress demonstrates how well it highlights her stylistic triumph. But by reiterating, again and again, how both are constructed artifices and by demonstrating the façade of fashionable success—and fashionable failure—Thackeray stays quite true to his prediction that his novel is one "without a hero." The absence of a "perfect" heroine and a "perfect" villainess helps to highlight the ambiguity and complexity of the construction of a fashionable female identity in the early Victorian era.

Mary Eliza Haweis, among other writers of her time, spent a great deal of energy and ink trying to convince her reading public that danger lurked where artificial fashions reigned. In her *The Art of Beauty*, she offers images similar to Thackeray's that work to exaggerate the fashions of the time in order to emphasize the problems they present to the natural female form. Her work presents women's bodies internally, with a look at the anatomical deformities that can occur with the current fashions.

When urging women to choose corsets that would be a "servant" rather than a "tyrant" in supporting the female figure, Haweis offers these comparative illustrations: in examination of the skeletal frame, "Fig. 9—Natural form of the ribs and spine" and "Fig. 10—Fashionable form of the ribs and spine" (49) and an examination of the anatomical frame, "Fig. 11—Natural position of the organs" and "Fig. 12—Deformed position of the organs" (50). These two sets of images show how the natural shape of the body has been manipulated through artificial means, namely, the corset, which was first brought to England, it seems, by either "Mademoiselle Pantine, a mistress of Marshal Saxe" or "an early Norman lady" (48), making the ancestry of corsetry, in Haweis's eyes, decidedly French. Therefore, as her illustrations demonstrate, it is the French we are to blame for these artificial deformities of the natural womanly shape, just as Becky Sharp's insistence on artificial beauty stands in stark contrast to Amelia Sedley's natural, more English looks. But it is important to remember that even Haweis advocates for supportive garments; her argument is not to abandon the corset—to do so, it seems, would be to "look very slovenly" (48)—but rather to find a garment that "aspir[es] to embrace" rather than "hugs like a bear—crushing in the ribs, injuring the lungs and heart, the stomach, and many other internal organs" (49). If we were to alter Thackeray's estimation, then, we can see that only women *and* corsetry know how to wound so. Even with this supporting device that embraces, the natural shape is altered, making Haweis's suggestion one for artificiality, however slight.

To be a fashionable success, then, is to be artificial; there is no "natural" style, despite English claims. What remains important to the English reader is whether that artificiality is evident. What Thackeray's novel seems to argue—and indeed, what many Victorian novels and fashion tracts seem to suggest—is that while artificiality is an undesirable trait, women can *learn* to seem natural. Ultimately, despite England's panicked insistence to the contrary, there is no difference between the way French and English women approach fashion. *Vanity Fair* sets up a dichotomy between Becky and Amelia and thus the dichotomy between French and English and between artificial and natural; it calls attention to the artifice of all fashionable persons and personas. When English writers claim "naturalness" for their countrywomen, they are in fact veiling artificiality and removing agency from a woman's understanding of fashion and her own body. Englishwomen should be "natural" because they should be symbolic representations of a national ideology that prides itself on the modesty and natural beauty of its women. If Amelia's "naturalness," discussed throughout Thackeray's novel, is a version of Becky's artifice, then the designation of "natural" is a false one. Thackeray's novel emphasizes Victorian England's concerns over the artificiality of women as well as its subsequent relegation of such artificiality to the French; Frenchwoman Becky Sharp is an artifice, a sham, because England needs her to be so.

Chapter Three

"The Will and Pleasure of Women"

The Feminine Love of Fashion in
George Eliot's *Middlemarch*

Not surprisingly, I have met with resistance during my career as people discount the power and effect of fashion. Do they do this because it is believed to be the province of women? Because to like so-called frivolous things must mean you are frivolous yourself? I have pondered these questions, and more, since I began my dissertation in the early 2000s. My work has been met with equal parts celebration and resistance, and, most surprisingly, the majority of the resistance has centered on George Eliot.

It was the chapter of my dissertation my committee disagreed with. It has been the most controversial of all my topics: to say George Eliot loves fashion, as seen in novels like *Middlemarch, Daniel Deronda*, and especially *Romola*. George Eliot is a "serious" novelist, not a romance or gothic author like Elizabeth Gaskell or even the Brontës. How could such a serious author write about such frivolous things? She rails against them in "Silly Novels by Lady Novelists" (1856) when she attacks the heroines who are "the ideal woman in feelings, faculties, and flounces" (443) and the authoresses of these novels who "write in elegant boudoirs, with violet-coloured ink and a ruby pen" (444). The George Eliot of our acclaim certainly is above writing such characters and in such a way. She writes, as Virginia Woolf reminds us, *Middlemarch,* which is "one of the few English novels written for grown-up people." Grown-up people don't read about clothes and don't enjoy reading about clothes, as evidenced by the scathing review against "mind-and-millinery novels" of 1856. Yet

George Eliot describes clothing again and again, talking about fashionable clothing and doing so in a loving manner.[1] Scholars from Kate Flint to Jean Arnold to Clair Hughes to Andrew H. Miller have all seen fit to write about this novel and its author's approach to materiality.[2] Why then do we resist the word "fashion" in conjunction with George Eliot?

I have a small but worthy cause I have fought for since I began graduate work, and that is to take issue with the privileging of so-called realist fiction over genre fiction in the academy. I think that people have discounted George Eliot's love of fashion precisely because she writes those novels "for grown-up people," which means something like realist fiction triumphing over genre as written by all the writers discussed thus far and further in this work. To say this, to believe this, is to ultimately say that fashion, as a subject in genre fiction, *is* frivolous when talked about by Gaskell or Thackeray, but not when discussed by a serious novelist like George Eliot. And once again, people take umbrage with genre and fashion precisely because they are the province of women. Saying George Eliot writes for "grown-up people" implies she writes for men, or at least women educated to think like men. These are novels that make you think, not novels that make you feel—another point I disagree with, because *Middlemarch* and *Romola* and *Daniel Deronda* all make me feel deeply. They are novels that *describe* clothing but do not revel in fashion. And to that I say these critics are wrong. George Eliot's careful presentation and deconstruction of clothing throughout her novels—for our intents and purposes, we are focusing on *Middlemarch*—shows a writer aware of fashion not only of her own era but also of those in the past. The research George Eliot conducted to write *Romola*,[3] for example, or to set *Middlemarch* in the 1830s rather than the 1880s meant that she had to look at clothing—if not the actual textiles, then books and fashion magazines about the clothing. And to carefully and lovingly present her characters' sartorial choices—Dorothea Brooke and Rosamond Vincy, in particular—is to speak to enjoyment of the fashions these clothes represent. Andrew H. Miller in *Novels Behind Glass* argues that:

> Eliot is clearly devaluing feminine material culture—it opposes "responsible" reason. Her discomfort with material culture arises from the ability, associated with the feminine, to operate beneath the notice of reason. While material culture can be associated with wider thoughts and cares, the connection is suspect. When Eliot does focus on material culture—training

the light of responsible reason on that unconsidered source of moods and habits—her concern is that which occupied us most fully in the first chapter: the alienation of people from the goods around them. (192)

I cite Miller here because he is representative of the resistance I have encountered whenever I discuss George Eliot and fashion. Throughout this chapter, I will show how Eliot actually appreciates the feminine and does so by creating characters worthy of our attention (Dorothea Brooke) and characters who manage to get their happy endings despite a frivolous love of fashion (Rosamond Vincy). Material culture, associated with the feminine, is actually valued by Eliot.[4]

I ask you to look at this 1858 photograph portrait of George Eliot, Mary Ann Evans, (housed in London's National Portrait Gallery) and

Figure 3.1. Photograph of George Eliot; after London Stereoscopic & Photographic Company; Mayall. *Source:* Courtesy of the National Portrait Gallery, London. Used with permission.

enjoy how fashion-forward Eliot is in it. She is wearing bell sleeves with large lace cuffs underneath. Her top is likely patterned with velvet strips, which continue down the cuff of her sleeves and the pattern on her skirt. The lace collar looks to be removeable and so able to be worn with other dresses. The preciousness of lace, both handmade and machine-made, would make a removeable lace collar a worthwhile investment. One need only remember the cat eating the lace soaking in milk in Gaskell's *Cranford* to understand the lengths women would go to in order to protect and keep their pieces of lace. There is texture in the material as seen on the sleeves when examined closely. And while this photograph is cut off at the waist, the original photograph shows more of Eliot's skirt, which is full and, since it is taken in 1858, likely with a crinoline. The horizontal stripes continue down the center of the skirt, and given the time period and the crinoline she is most likely wearing, this is a two- or three-piece outfit.

Figure 3.2. More Detailed Photograph of George Eliot; after London Stereoscopic & Photographic Company; Mayall. *Source:* Courtesy of the National Portrait Gallery, London. Used with permission.

Most extraordinarily, she is smiling, although it is said she did not enjoy this photograph of herself. The dress is the epitome of a late-1850s dress, and Eliot wears it well. The pose, while awkward, is coquettish and feminine, two traits that Eliot is definitely not associated with.[5] Perhaps Eliot didn't like this photograph of herself for precisely those reasons: that she, rather than her characters, would be seen as feminine, as interested in fashion. Surely it is this seriousness of Eliot, and the fact that she disliked such a fashion-forward photograph of herself, that is to blame for scholars not believing in Eliot's love of fashion in her novels.[6]

But the textual evidence is there. Ellen Moers, in *Literary Women: The Great Writers*, states that Dorothea Brooke "has what must be the most stunning wardrobe in Victorian fiction" (195), a point with which I wholeheartedly agree. Dorothea's wardrobe is gorgeous, rich and full, despite the rather plain presentations, all materials are fine and well-made. She is not the flashy Rosamond or snaky Gwendolyn, although I also argue that both characters enjoy their share of support from Eliot as well. She is, seemingly, "Quakerish" in her dress, as some have argued before me.[7] But rather, I see Dorothea as appreciating fine things, as evidenced by her actions in the novel again and again. Krista Lysack argues that "Dorothea undergoes a number of extraordinary costume changes throughout the novel" (100) and that her clothing is both "at once anachronistic and ahead of its time. A style that seems to belong to no particular era or fad, it is nevertheless the result of [a] residual relation to the consumer world it would seem to ignore" (101).

Middlemarch does not cast judgment on its female characters for their seemingly excessive love of finery. Rather, its utter admiration of Dorothea Brooke, a character traditionally defined by her selflessness, and its more ambivalent portrayal of Rosamond Vincy, a character traditionally defined by her selfishness, offer two sketches of women's responses to and love of dress. Dorothea, seemingly unfashionable and contrary, is in fact very stylish and has complete control and awareness of the most flattering clothing for her body and coloring.[8] Rosamond, on the other hand, appears to be shallow, superficial, and vain, but Eliot's portrayal of her is bittersweet and ambivalent about the social expectations of fashionable womanhood. Her love of clothing does not cause her unhappiness in the end. Rather, the novel's complicated conclusion of Rosamond as the wife of a wealthy, doting, and aging husband offers Rosamond exactly what she wanted throughout the novel: wealth and materiality. While Eliot's novel by no means establishes Rosamond as an equal counterpart to the pure-intentioned and complex Dorothea Brooke, the novel's constant attentions to both women's fashionability or antifashionability and, most interestingly, both women's love of finery offer an alternative to the traditional narrative that insists a woman's love of fashion is a socially expected but still socially abhorred trait. Further, *Middlemarch* argues that fashion and dress are arenas through which women gain access to and occupy a place of feminine power and through which women achieve agency and control over their own bodies without damaging the national character of England.

Admiration of Self and Others: Reading the Fashioned Body

On October 15, 1861, the *Daily News* published an article on "A Real Social Evil," in which Harriet Martineau argues against the very popular crinoline, which is at the height of fashion in the 1860s, and recounts several serious and even fatal injuries caused to both wearers of the crinoline and passersby.[9] Martineau notes that "Nothing can be more distasteful to us, and to many others who will say 'Amen!' to the comment of this jury than the petty tyranny which overbears the will and pleasure of women in regard to their dress, or which annoys them in their proper work and amusement of arranging themselves according to their own taste and convenience" (33). Martineau begins her plea by offering a common bond between herself and her reader. Both of "us" are intelligent and rational, and therefore both of "us" can see the ridiculousness of a fashion that, as Martineau reminds us, originated in France (34). Martineau blames these French fashions for more than the sway they hold over Englishwomen; she argues that the crinoline and hoop popularized in France and followed by all women "senselessly" is an "evil" which is "responsible for more deaths . . . than any other fashion ever caused" (34). She also sees outside influence over a woman's fashion as a "petty tyranny which overbears the will and pleasure of women in regard to their dress" and the acquiescence to the current trend of the crinoline to be contrary to "their own taste and convenience." For Martineau, French influence over English dress is not solely to blame for the popularity and seeming permanence of the crinoline. Rather, Englishwomen's conformity to current fashion trends is to blame. For Martineau, a woman's strong-mindedness and independence are best demonstrated in her ability to display herself fashionably and well, according to her "own taste and convenience," not the taste and convenience of society at large. Most nineteenth-century English writers saw women's work in the creation and maintenance of fashion to be detrimental to women's health, women's morality, and, ultimately, women's characters. As an adoration of fashion becomes for a nineteenth-century audience an excessive love of finery, and thus an excessive love of the artificial construction of female bodies, a love of fashion signals a woman's excessive vanity. Declaring fashion to be an "amusement" that can in fact be considered "proper work" that depends upon the "will and pleasure of women," Martineau justifies feminine interest in dress and counters these traditional equations of a woman's love of finery with selfishness and vanity.[10] Fashion is, for Martineau, a woman's concern, and autonomy over her own fashion and by extension her own body is a woman's right. With this declaration, Martineau establishes that dress and, more specifically, fashionable dress are important components of women's lives.

Martineau concludes her piece with a call to queen and country, in which she asks her countrywomen to "follow the royal example which we anticipate" (37) of decrying the crinoline, as Queen Victoria exhibits rationality in the decisions about fashion for herself and for the royal household. Even if Queen Victoria does not outlaw the crinoline overtly, Martineau still insists that her countrywomen "act without [the royal decree] in that sphere of home in which every English matron is a queen" (37). In her estimation, the home and England are synonymous; by stating that "every English matron is a queen," Martineau states that the home over which this queen rules is her nation. In a discussion of women's fashionable choices that urges them to consider their "own taste and convenience," Martineau's understanding of the home as nation makes every fashionable choice a significant one, weighted with national import. An English woman is the queen of her home, and her home is both the home, that physical place of residence, and the Home, the country in which she lives. Martineau never denounces fashion itself and instead views it a female "amusement" that is important enough to deserve a call to queen and country; in this equation, Martineau supports a woman's interest in fashion as socially and nationally acceptable, as long as it is "according to [women's] own taste and convenience." She urges women to make autonomous choices in their fashions to demonstrate the rationality she expects of her countrywomen and to use "their own free will" (37) in matters of dress. Even if her queen does not outlaw the crinoline directly, Martineau trusts Englishwomen to act rationally in their own homes, that place "in which every English matron is a queen." Despite her vehemence against the crinoline, Martineau appreciates fashion and dress and wishes her countrywomen to do the same. Her call to queen and country in a discussion of fashion expresses the importance of fashion to the English nation at large.

Like *Cranford*, *Middlemarch* is set in the 1830s just before the reform debates change the face of England, and, like *Cranford*, *Middlemarch* establishes economy of dress as a socially acceptable response to monetary troubles. Dorothea's plain dress could be attributed to the "well-bred economy, which in those days made show in dress the first item to be deducted from, when any margin was required for expenses more distinctive of rank" (33), which would support the book's assertion that Dorothea is tasteful in style and in substance. By avoiding showiness, the elegance of economy the Cranford Amazons also practice, Dorothea and the people of Middlemarch who avoid "show in dress" demonstrate their good taste in not overdressing around those who, financially, cannot.[11] The narration also very carefully tells us that "Such reasons would have been enough to account for plain dress, quite apart from religious feeling; but in Miss Brooke's case, religion alone would have determined it" (33).[12] For Dorothea, economy is not the reason for her relatively plain dress, nor is just the "pride of being ladies" (33). Her plain dress is according to her personal choice, not according to her domestic economy or her class status, which the novel tells us is "not exactly aristocratic" but still "unquestionably 'good' " (33). Dorothea's sister, Celia, wears dress that, in contrast to her sister's, has "a shade of coquetry in its arrangements" (33), but this dress differs from Dorothea's only slightly. Celia wears "scarcely more trimmings" than Dorothea, and "it was only to close observers that her dress differed from her sister's" (33). Understanding that fashion and dress are, by their very nature, made to be visible, Dorothea and Celia avoid the side-by-side comparison of "plain garments" and "provincial fashion." The rather plain garments Dorothea wears complement her body, her posture, her coloring, and her beauty; as her sister, Celia must resemble Dorothea at least slightly.[13] Therefore, the two women's similar dress is complementary to them both, and Celia's "shade of coquetry in [her dress's] arrangements" offers further emphasis of the choice both women demonstrate over their clothing.

Although Eliot declares herself to be rather judgmental of "silly novels by lady novelists," particularly those of the "*mind-and-millinery* species" with a heroine who is "usually an heiress [. . . who] is perfectly well-dressed and perfectly religious" (90) among other designators, Dorothea is seemingly all three. Yet both Dorothea's contrariness in fashion and her personal style offer an alternative to the "mind-and-millinery" novels that Eliot denigrates. While *Middlemarch* is interested in the clothing of its female characters, it is less interested in *what* their fashionable choices are than *why*; Eliot details the intricacies of dress and fashion in order to argue for the taste, style, and fashionable autonomy of women in contrast to a national standard that understands women's love of dress as simple vanity and the antithesis of English womanhood. When the Brooke sisters first explore and divide up their mother's jewels among themselves, Dorothea's taste and ability to accessorize fashion to best suit a woman's beauty is revealed to be applicable not only to her own body but also to the bodies of other women. When she opens the jewelry box, Dorothea "immediately took up the necklace" of "purple amethysts set in exquisite gold work" and "fastened it round her sister's neck, where it fitted almost as closely as a bracelet; but the circle suited the Henrietta-Maria style of Celia's head and neck," and tells her sister that she must "wear that with your Indian muslin" (38). Dorothea recognizes that the shape of Celia's head and neck was popular in the seventeenth century, and the choker style of the necklace would complement Celia's shape and would emphasize her neck when worn with a lighter gown like the Indian muslin.[14] Also, Dorothea knows intimately the contents of Celia's wardrobe; while the Brooke sisters are not extremely wealthy, they are not of an economic status that would necessitate only one or two dresses. While we cannot assume either Celia's or Dorothea's wardrobe to be plentiful, we can assume that both women have their fair share of clothing, as the descriptions of the women's dress frequently change in the novel. In short, Dorothea knows her fashion.[15]

Dorothea and Celia enjoy not only the beautiful jewelry left to them by their mother but also the act of appreciating fashion together. Dorothea's ability to instantly recognize what would be both attractive and complementary on another woman argues for her understanding of fashion. Further, the novel refuses to determine either Dorothea or Celia as excessively vain for their attention to details of dress and, in particular, the accessorizing of dress.[16] The novel immediately establishes Dorothea as exemplary of womanly and Christian virtue, so when she exhibits what her sister views as a "weakness" (39) for an emerald ring and bracelet, Dorothea is in fact exhibiting her strength. She recognizes that the emeralds are the finest jewels in the box, and that they suit her best. Dorothea exhibits both her taste and her recognition of her own style in this moment. By taking the finest jewels in the box, she takes those of the best quality. But by taking them because they suit her best, she demonstrates that her taste is of the finest quality. Also, Dorothea acknowledges that the very act of wearing the emeralds is enjoyable; when she returns to her work, she does not remove the jewels, and "She thought of often having them by her, to feed her eye at these little fountains of pure colour" (39). The language of this passage suggests Dorothea's female vanity from her enjoyment of the emeralds, even when her sister's jealousy causes her to ask if Dorothea intends to wear the elaborate jewels in public (39). While Dorothea and Celia may think Dorothea is above the pettiness of vanity, in fact she is not; rather, the language of the passage offers the vision of beautiful things, those "little fountains of pure colour," as an acceptable reason for what some may deem as vanity. The emeralds are described as natural and vital to survival; Dorothea does not just enjoy the emerald ring and bracelet but will "feed her eye" with them.[17] Further, Dorothea's moment of vanity is subsumed by her superior taste. She does not take "her full share of jewels" (40), which Celia is angry over, but rather only the ones that complement her best.[18]

Dorothea's taste in and discernment of both fashion and people are reiterated throughout the text, and while her choices are often seen as contrary, they are decidedly autonomous. The most interesting choices for Dorothea come in her fashions, and even her choice of hairstyle is dependent on its becoming nature rather than its popularity. Dorothea is determined to wear what is most flattering to herself. She "wore her brown hair flatly braided and coiled behind so as to expose the outline of her head in a daring manner at a time when public feeling required the meagreness of nature to be dissimulated by tall barricades of frizzed curls and bows, never surpassed by any great race except the Feejeean" (50). Her hairstyle is described in terms of revelation and shock; Dorothea wears her hair specifically "to expose the outline of her head" in what at the time was considered to be "a daring manner." This exposure's daring quality is precisely its revelation of the naturalness of the shape of her head; Dorothea does not hide the "meagreness" of nature, a short forehead or unflatteringly shaped brow, by "tall barricades of frizzed curls and bows," which the novel equates not with England but with a foreign race. In this moment, then, the hairstyle Dorothea chooses to wear is, by default, more English than the hairstyles currently popular in England.

Dorothea's "daring manner" in her hairstyle is daring not only because it exposes the naturalness of her body in a way that best pleases Dorothea but also because it is not the commonly accepted fashion for women's hair. In this moment, Dorothea's choice of personal style over what is fashionable is emphasized, and Eliot argues that personal style, what Martineau would call a woman's "own taste and convenience," is not a rejection of social mores. Rather, it is an assertion of women's power and autonomy in the fashionable arena and, further, in the English nation at large. Eliot's novel rejects Victorian ideology for womanhood throughout its plot, and does so in order to best demonstrate that Dorothea's personal choices—in fashion, in business, and in love—may be disastrous to her, but they are not disastrous to the social or national landscape of the time. Dorothea rejects fashion in favor of stylistic choice. By examining this through the lens of fashion or, in Dorothea's case, antifashion, we can see that fashion is as important to Eliot as it is to other women novelists of the time. The personal choices that Dorothea makes in her own dress could be considered unfashionable in that she does not always follow the fashion trends of the 1830s, but it is not because Dorothea is unaware of those fashions. To be unfashionable is to be unaware of fashionable trends. Rather, Dorothea is antifashionable because she is not ignorant of the prevailing fashions but rather rejects them outright in favor of dress more flattering to her beauty.[19] In Eliot's novel, Dorothea's taste and personal style are held in higher esteem than socially decreed fashionable dress and are, in Eliot's presentation, what fashion should ultimately be.[20] In this presentation of Dorothea, then, Eliot, like Martineau, understands dress not as an arena of judgment for women but rather an arena of power for women.[21]

The novel emphasizes Dorothea's beauty and her taste, both of which are traits that serve her well throughout the novel as she makes personal decisions regarding dress accordingly.[22] In her work *Dressed in Fiction*, Clair Hughes argues that "Dressing is one activity that Dorothea can control. Unwilling to conform to gender codes that correlate femininity to external ornament, her appearance can be read as a dissenting experiment in self-representation and therefore arguably egoistic playacting" (94).[23] While I agree that "dress is one activity that Dorothea can control" and that control comes as an unwillingness to conform, I think her dress is too important to view only in terms of a refusal of gender conformity. Rather, Dorothea's dressing is a purposeful attention to fashion, rather than an outright rejection of it. Like the women in the fashionable advertisements that Sharon Marcus studies, Dorothea has the power to look and the power to look back. Unlike Becky Sharp, Dorothea does not use that fashionable power to belittle other women but, rather, to express commonality and, most importantly for Dorothea, love. In sharing the jewelry with Celia, for example, and noting the most flattering dresses Celia should wear with each piece, Dorothea demonstrates that in Eliot's estimation, admiring and enjoying fashion is not a signal of female vanity. Rather, it is an expression of what Martineau believes is the "will and pleasure of women." Dorothea, therefore, is not the martyred character that her "plain garments" might otherwise suggest; she is a beautiful woman who understands the construction and dissemination of beauty.

In fact, most of the oddness attributed to Dorothea's dress is in her decisive dressing for the benefit of herself and other women, not for men. At a dinner party prior to her wedding to Casaubon, Dorothea wears a "silver-gray dress—the simple lines of her dark-brown hair parted over her brow and coiled massively behind, in keeping with the entire absence from her manner and expression of all search after mere effect" (96). Gray is a common color for Dorothea and one that is very flattering to her form and coloring. On her honeymoon, in fact, she wears "Quakerish gray drapery" that causes Will Ladislaw and his artistic companion to admire her (176).[24] Her hairstyle, too, is typical of her standard dress, as the "simple lines" of it emphasize her face, and the coil of hair "massively behind" her head emphasizes the delicacy of her neck. But the narration's notice that absent from "her manner and expression" was the "search after mere effect" argues that Dorothea wears this style precisely because it offers her enjoyment, not because she wishes others to admire her. Dorothea wears this clothing like she chooses the emerald jewelry: because she gains personal enjoyment from them. Clothing is, for Dorothea, a personal expression and a pleasant sensation. When one man of her acquaintance notices that she is "an uncommonly fine woman, by God!" (97), his companion responds that she is "not my style of woman: I like a woman who lays herself out a little more to please us" (97). Here, Eliot directly equates the construction of a woman's dress and outward self with the social belief that women dress beautifully for men. In dressing for herself, in experiencing pleasure solely from wearing the clothing she wishes to wear, Dorothea contradicts the common social expectations for women's clothing. She denies the commonly held assumptions of women's vanity—her attention to dress is often misunderstood as an inattention—and she denies the commonly held assumptions of women's fashionable choices: she dresses as Martineau urges all Englishwomen to dress, according to her own taste, amusement, and style. Eliot creates a new standard of beauty with Dorothea in creating a female character that understands the social expectations of fashion but instead chooses to please her eyes, her senses, and her self.

Also at the dinner party is Rosamond Vincy, the character who represents the opposite ideal of womanhood from Dorothea and who is in this scene held up as the more beautiful and desirable woman of the two.[25] One of the men in this conversation declares that he prefers his women "blond, with a certain gait, and a swan neck. . . . If I were a marrying man I should choose Miss Vincy before either of [the Brooke sisters]" (98). Rosamond is the most socially fashionable woman in the text. Her dress is of such "fit and fashion" that "no dressmaker could look at it without emotion" (353). Rosamond fulfills the social expectations for fashion; when "no dressmaker could look" at her dress "without emotion," the dressmaker sees Rosamond's potential for displaying fashion, not fashion's potential for highlighting Rosamond. The novel's ultimate comparison of the two women argues that fashionably conscious Rosamond and antifashionable but stylish Dorothea are two representations of the female love of fashion. While Dorothea's personal style is antifashionable for the time, she understands female aestheticism. Rosamond, too, understands female aestheticism and the social expectations for unmarried women of her beauty and class. Unlike Dorothea, however, Rosamond embraces the social understanding of women as beautiful objects and sees herself as an "exquisite ornament" (464).

Rosamond's understanding of herself as beautiful is in part due to her "excellent taste in costume" (103) and her understanding of her own body. Even when walking into a room Rosamond enters "bearing up her riding-habit with much grace" (112), demonstrating that she understands how her body moves within clothing and, in short, how her body moves. She has "a habitual gesture with her as pretty as any movements of a kitten's paw" of reaching up "her hand to touch her wondrous hair-plaits" (151). Like Amelia Sedley, Rosamond learns the movement, style, and grace socially understood as the province of beautiful women at school; she learns her more kittenish movements during her education at Mrs. Lemon's (151), and thus understands the artificiality in the construction of female beauty. Even when she takes off her hat, she "adjust[s] her veil, and applie[s] little touches of her finger-tips to her hair" (115). Rosamond is constantly aware of how her body fits in and understands fashion and also of how best to figure herself to be beautiful. When Dorothea pays her visit to the new Mrs. Lydgate, Rosamond welcomes the attention because "What is the use of being exquisite if you are not seen by the best judges?" (353). Rosamond understands Dorothea to be "one of those country divinities not mixing with Middlemarch mortality" (353). When compared to Dorothea and her simple yet utterly flattering antifashionable dress, Rosamond naturally is viewed as just as beautiful but too well put together. Not only is Rosamond's dress so perfect that the dressmaker would weep, but her "large embroidered collar" was worn precisely so that "all beholders would know the price of" it, and her "controlled self-consciousness of manner" is described as the "expensive substitute for simplicity" (353). Here, Eliot establishes that Rosamond's faults are not in her fashions but in her fashionability; she has learned what it is to be fashionable from her school, from her society, and from her peers. Like Dorothea, Rosamond understands what is flattering on her; unlike Dorothea, Rosamond does not make her own fashionable choices. Her awareness of fashion trends and details of dress make her choices for her. Rosamond can construct a beautiful attractive self, but she cannot compete with Dorothea for independence of thought in dress. In this sense, then, Rosamond is the more nationally desirable ideal of womanhood, while Dorothea, and not Rosamond, is the more fashionably avant-garde woman of the two.

The novel recognizes Rosamond's awareness of the construction of womanhood and femininity, arguing that she was "not one of those helpless girls who betray themselves unawares, and whose behaviour is awkwardly driven by their impulses, instead of being steered by wary grace and propriety" (234). Eliot establishes "wary grace and propriety" as the artificial construction of womanhood and contrasts it with more natural awkward impulses. But Eliot is not disapproving of Rosamond's self-construction or the fact that she never "showed any unbecoming knowledge, and was always that combination of correct sentiments, music, dancing, drawing, elegant note-writing, private album for extracted verse, and perfect blond loveliness" (235), all the required accomplishments for a young lady of Rosamond's class position. Instead, the narrative entreats the reader to:

> Think no unfair evil of her, pray: she had no wicked plots, nothing sordid or mercenary; in fact, she never thought of money except as something necessary which other people would always provide. She was not in the habit of devising falsehoods, and if her statements were no direct clue to fact, why, they were not intended in that light—they were among her elegant accomplishments, intended to please. Nature had

> inspired many arts in finishing Mrs Lemon's favorite pupil,
> who by general consent . . . was a rare compound of beauty,
> cleverness, and amiability. (235)

These estimations of Rosamond's worth are gently mocking of Rosamond but more scathing about the so-called accomplishments offered to women of Rosamond's class, age, and status. Rosamond has the benefits of beauty and cleverness, but she does not have the benefits of social expectation. Because she is beautiful, she is more prone to the "many arts in finishing" at Mrs. Lemon's school. By never showing "any unbecoming knowledge," Rosamond always fits neatly into a paradigm of early nineteenth-century womanhood best defined by the litany of talents, such as music, drawing, or "perfect blond loveliness." She is the height of English womanhood, and she is to be pitied for it.

The language of this passage, however, emphasizes an alternative to traditional understandings of fashionable, accomplished women. While the novel still compares Dorothea and Rosamond and ultimately finds Rosamond wanting, *Middlemarch* sympathizes with the few recourses Rosamond has. She is not "wicked," "sordid or mercenary," and therefore the reader should "think no unfair evil of her." If she happened to tell falsehoods, they were not devised but rather ignorant of fact. *Middlemarch* insists that Rosamond's vanity is not evil. Rather, Rosamond's desire for beautiful things is all she knows, as her understanding of herself as a beautiful thing or an "exquisite ornament to the drawing-room" (464) is all she knows. *Middlemarch* pities Rosamond for this reason and voices a maid's internal monologue that notes "there never did anybody look so pretty in a bonnet, poor thing" when Rosamond walks by "in her walking dress" (594). Her prettiness, superior to anyone else's, is a cause for sympathy even from the servants. And even the servants recognize that Rosamond's beauty is dependent on her ability to dress herself; Rosamond is not pretty solely due to nature but, rather, is pretty "in a bonnet." She is beautiful only because she is able to dress as her society expects her to dress.

Eliot's presentation of Rosamond is dependent on the character's learned construction and development of fashion, but Rosamond's fashionable self is the national standard of beauty. As we have seen with many Victorian texts, like *Cranford*, references to fashion are intertwined with references to France, and in *Middlemarch*, suggestions that Rosamond aligns herself with French ideas and fashions is spoken not through narration but through the conversation of gossiping Middlemarch matriarchs. After the murder scandal involving Mr. Bulstrode, the women of Middlemarch note that the family will probably "go and live abroad somewhere," as "that is what is generally done when there is anything disgraceful in a family" (576). They express sympathy for his wife, Harriet, who "wears very neat patterns always" and always "wishes to do right" to her society through her fashion (576). Despite Harriet's enjoyment of dress, the Middlemarch women do not believe that she will enjoy France, arguing "how hard it will be for her to go among foreigners" (576). While Harriet's attention to fashion is forgivable, even though she and her daughters "had new Tuscan bonnets" on in church the day before, the same cannot be said for her niece, Rosamond. The women of Middlemarch note that many believe Rosamond's husband, Lydgate, "ought to have kept among the French," which would "suit *her* well enough, I dare say" as there is "that kind of lightness about her. But she got that from her mother; she never got it from her aunt Bulstrode, who always gave her good advice, and to my knowledge would rather have had her marry elsewhere" (576, emphasis original). The "kind of lightness about" Rosamond is in the context of the conversation seemingly rooted in Rosamond's attention to fashion, even at the expense of her husband's well-being and character.[26] Eliot ultimately connects Rosamond's national standard of womanhood—fashionable, beautiful, vain, and superficial—with the very Frenchness the English standard of female beauty supposedly abhors.

Eliot's conclusion about an Englishwoman's love of fashion is not a decree against female vanity or an abhorrence of the French influence over English fashion. Rather, her ambivalent ending for Rosamond—happy in a marriage to a wealthy, elderly gentleman—gives Rosamond everything she has longed for throughout the novel. Her conclusion is the "very pretty show" she made with "her daughters, driving out in her carriage" (638). Antifashionable Dorothea is happy in the end, as well, rejecting the wealthy life so many others wanted for her in order to marry Will Ladislaw. So, too, does she seemingly reject dress, as she tells Will, "I want so little—no new clothes" (622). Of course Dorothea does not want new clothes; she never has, as she is quite happy with the clothing she already owns. Ultimately, *Middlemarch* loves fashion as much as I argue George Eliot herself did,[27] and in its construction of women's genuine interest in dress, Eliot's novel argues that a woman's love of fashion and, further, her understanding of dress and how best to complement her body and her beauty is not a signal of vanity, or the first step toward a sexual fall, or even reason for national concern. Eliot, like Martineau, sees that the "petty tyranny which overbears the will and pleasure of women in regard to their dress" (33) is what forces the social understanding of women's love of fashion to mere vanity. For Eliot, Martineau, and, to no small extent, Gaskell, the "petty tyranny which overbears" women and their attention to and love of fashion and dress is the social and national expectations for English womanhood. As the next chapter will show, the nineteenth century's understanding of women's use and manipulation of fashion will reach its critical point during the suffrage movement, when militant and nonmilitant protesters alike use and manipulate fashion to communicate the national role they are denied as women.

Chapter Four

"Now She's All Hat and Ideas"

Fashioning the British Suffrage Movement

Figure 4.1. Black Silk Stockings Worn by the Suffragette Lillian Burslem. *Source:* Courtesy of the London Museum. Used with permission.

These innocuous black silk stockings[1] were embroidered by Mrs. Lilian Burslem to be worn at suffrage marches in the early twentieth century.[2] Something so personal and private, to be held up with a garter under a woman's dress, are embroidered with the phrase "VOTES FOR WOMEN" and the symbolic colors purple, green, and white for the Women's Social and

Political Union (WSPU), the militant arm of the women's suffrage movement.[3] I remark on their personal and private nature because they would be under a dress, not necessarily meant to be seen. Why then embroider them with "VOTES FOR WOMEN" and the colors of the WSPU? Suffragettes were asked to wear the colors in public, shop at suffragette-friendly stores, and subscribe to suffragette-friendly fashion magazines. Despite popular belief that the suffragettes eschewed fashion—one often imagines not a fashionable Edwardian woman but rather a termagant in bloomers—the suffragettes were encouraged to wear fashionable clothing and present a unified beautiful presence at their marches. Photographs and postcards from the time reveal that suffragettes wore their working-class uniforms (the Lancashire lass), their national costumes (Welsh, Irish, Scottish, and Indian), or simply their Sunday best, as we see so often with English suffragettes. So many of these fashions are publicly revealed and seen. Why then embroider the very private stockings?

Throughout this book we've dealt with fashions both private and public, and, ultimately, the question then becomes why? Why make something so private so very publicly a spectacle? The chances of an Edwardian woman displaying that much leg so her stockings are read by the public are minuscule, unless it is revealed against her will—while being carried away from a protest by a policeman perhaps. But of the fashions we've seen and handled throughout this book—the reform corset, the red crinoline—nothing demonstrates more political and national savvy than these very private black silk stockings. Wearing the call for the vote so close to her body, one imagines Mrs. Lilian Burslem to be proud of her embroidery, showing off these very private stockings to her fellow suffragettes. Perhaps the embroidery brought her some comfort if she was arrested at a protest march and taken to Holloway Prison. To see the colors, something beautiful in prison, may have brought her peace and hope.

Public and private were meant to be divided well into the early twentieth century, and it isn't until the work the suffragettes did in World War I was finished and acknowledged that they were granted the right to vote. During the early twentieth century, through the most militant activism of the women's suffrage movement, the suffragettes practiced what Barbara Green calls "performative activism," which was "the spectacle of women present[ing] itself both as an effective method of organized rebellion and as a problem to feminist activists" (68): effective because it garnered them attention but problematic because of public displays of violence, like breaking windows or setting buildings on fire (Green 68).

But even before that the suffragettes crashed public and private together, protesting against the lack of representation and the vote, and they did so with their clothing and their mouths and their bodies. Hunger strikes, imprisonment, shopping at suffragette-friendly stores, and wearing representative colors of the suffrage movement, they literally wrote the fight onto their bodies again and again.

The common belief about the lack of fashionable women in the early feminist movement was most certainly perpetrated by "Opponents of the movement [who] have almost universally represented the suffragist as a dowd, caring nothing for dress" (Nita 87). In her 5 November 1909 *Votes for Women* column, "The World We Live In: On Frocks and Other Things," Nita argues that, in fact, "It would be nearer the truth, probably, to say that the suffragist giving scope to her intellect is of all women the best fitted to express her own individuality in the clothes she wears" (87). By presenting these two stereotypes side by side, the fashionable flirt and the unfashionable dowd, Nita highlights the hypocrisy in assumptions about women and fashion: caring too much for dress marks a woman as ignorant of politics, and caring about politics marks a woman as ignorant of dress. William J. F. Keenan argues that "dress is clearly neither culturally nor politically neutral. It is loaded with significance" (181), which early feminists understood completely. Suffragettes took full advantage of any implications of political position in their personal dress and public discussions of fashion. By publishing this fashion column alongside advertisements for fashionable and smart clothing, the editors of *Votes for Women* fully establish the importance of displaying a fashionable self to the cause.[4] Supporters of the WSPU demonstrated that a feminine concern for dress was not solely relegated to the middle-class home or domestic space, or to the women with the leisure and luxury to purchase new fashions. It was, in fact, a concern of *all* women, rich and poor, working and middle class, even those protesting their lack of vote, because like the very cause these women fought for, the fundamentals of dress and its trends bound women together. We can see that it bound together these early feminists especially, as they were the women most likely to be accused of eschewing femininity and their womanhood.

Suffragettes recognized the usefulness of fashion in conveying a woman's voice: they shopped at designated, marketed, and recognized "suffragette-friendly" stores, wrote fashion columns alongside their peaceful and militant action journalism, and otherwise identified themselves as activists for the vote by wearing specifically chosen, easily recognizable uniform colors that spoke of the movement they supported.[5] Critics such as Katrina Rolley and Joel H. Kaplan and Sheila Stowell have argued that this uniformity was coupled with the conscious feminization of the suffragettes' appearance. Many early women's rights activists, in order to fight more successfully for the vote, domesticated themselves to the ideals of late Victorian and Edwardian womanhood.[6] Kaplan and Stowell note that early feminists redefined the public/private divide to insist upon a distinctive feminine voice, thus making "dressing fashionably . . . a political act" (153).[7] Through an examination of imagery from the historical suffrage campaign and a novel by H. G. Wells, *Ann Veronica* (1909), I argue that the suffragettes' goals were not only fashionably feminine but also nationally fashionable. In order to present their allegiance to the English nation, the suffragettes concluded that the most moderate means of achieving their dual goals of the vote and of their nation's public support was to emphasize their fashionability and their nationality. Participating in the national landscape of England constructed them as good women and, moreover, good *English* women. By dressing carefully, fashionably, and well, suffragettes masqueraded their otherwise contentious political beliefs through the acceptable clothing of the middle and upper middle classes. This masquerade legitimized their roles as good Englishwomen and thus confirmed their rightful place within their nation, as well as bolstering their demands for equal citizenship through the vote.

"Strength and Honour Are Her Clothing"[8]: Suffrage, Nationalism, and Fashion

Discussions of fashion and politics such as the ones we've seen in early and mid-nineteenth-century texts pave the way for later discussions as fashion itself becomes overtly political toward the end of the nineteenth century and the beginning of the twentieth. Women's suffragists (members of the NUWSS, the National Union of Women's Suffrage Societies) and suffragettes (members of the WSPU) recognized the usefulness of fashion in conveying a woman's voice and often identified themselves as activists for the vote by wearing specifically chosen, easily recognizable uniform colors that spoke of the movement they supported.[9] Katrina Rolley reminds us that "garments and details of appearance were used to signal deviation from or adherence to the feminine ideal" (51). When the suffragettes used fashion, they attempted to look as much like the

Victorian and Edwardian ideal of womanhood as possible in order to adhere to standards of femininity.

As is now well documented, the suffragettes' and suffragists' campaigns relied heavily on spectacle to bring attention to their cause and, in the end, achieve women's suffrage. Militant and nonmilitant alike, women's rights activists participated in parades and demonstrations publicly and dressed fashionably privately in order to further their cause. Much has been written on the "purple, white, and green" color uniformity campaign of the WSPU; critics such as Lisa Tickner, Diane Atkinson, and Katrina Rolley extensively discuss the spectacle of color and the uniformity of dress of the suffragettes. But while discussions of the color campaigns are important and indeed plentiful, so, too, is the impact of national dress on the suffrage movement. For these large-scale parades, demonstrations, and spectacles, some suffragettes would wear the national dress unique to their countries of birth. For the British suffragettes, England, Wales, Scotland, and Ireland were represented in national costume, and even women from countries in the British Empire like India would participate in the demonstrations.[10] These activists used national dress to represent the political voice that the women of Britain did not have; by wearing the specific and recognizable national dress of their countries, these women demonstrated that they, too, occupied an important place in the construction and continuation of nationhood that was equal to the place of their male contemporaries.

Careful attention to dress went a long way in supporting the women's movement; the clothing stereotypically associated with suffragettes, whether mannish, odd dress or even prison uniforms distinguished the suffragettes from the potentially hostile viewing audience. Wearing fashionable clothing or even common everyday dress helped to erase any artificial distinctions between the suffragettes and the women they wanted to reach. When Emmeline Pankhurst, founder of the WSPU, negotiated on behalf of imprisoned suffragettes, she demanded that each arrested woman be accorded the same treatment as previous male political prisoners, including the right of the prisoner to wear her own clothing.[11] This concession, small as it may seem, helped morale among the women imprisoned in Holloway, the prison now famous for incarcerating several suffragettes. Suffragette Leonora Tyson, writing home to her sister, notes, "And the other day, when I was fetching water, a lady said—oh, thank you so much for your pretty dress! It is such a pleasure to see something pretty in this ugly place!" (Museum of London, *Prison Letters*).[12] From her letter, there is no way of knowing whether the lady is another suf-fragette, but even if she is not, Tyson has succeeded in forwarding the cause for women's suffrage by offering a "pretty" presentation of herself, boosting morale of a fellow inmate, and by still appearing feminine while incarcerated. Even in prison, some suffragettes are careful not to lose the appearance of femininity.

While her pretty dress lifted the spirits of another inmate, it seems that wearing her own clothes did the same for Tyson. The familiarity of the garments, even the scent of them, could possibly remind Tyson of home. Further, wearing her own clothes would help to lessen the fact that she was, in fact, incarcerated; her own clothes would continue to represent her fight for women's suffrage in a prison in which all other inmates, those not arrested for suffrage protesting, would not be afforded the same courtesy or would not be treated as a political prisoner. In the same letter, Tyson asks her sister for the following: "Please send me my white voile blouse (the old, old one) which is put away in a brown box under the mahogany table in the dormer room—and if possible, return the crepe blouse enclosed herewith. I cannot face the new pyjamas—so will you also send one of my old muslin nighties which are in a card-board box in the box room" (Museum of London, *Prison Letters*). Clothing requests of family members written from prison are not uncommon, in part thanks to the negotiations perpetrated by Mrs. Pankhurst. Suffragettes would send home their soiled linen for laundering and request specific articles of clothing in return. Suffragette Myra Sadd Brown even suggested to her husband that he bypass the prison surveillance system regulating correspondence by smuggling in a reply to her letter in the hem of the blue skirt she requested he send.[13]

Requests such as these reiterate the importance of personal clothing to these women, as well as their desire for familiar, comfortable items. While not as fashionable or as pretty because of its age, the "white voile blouse (the old, old one)" offers an image of comfort—a familiar item from home and an image of practicality—in prison, it is far more desirable to lose or soil an old blouse than a new one. Here, the suffragette is not fashion-forward or prettily put together; she is a practical woman and her casual comfort wear is familiar and rational. There is also another practical reason: as voile and muslin are made primarily of cotton, they would be cooler and would breathe more than a silk crepe and also would be easier to clean.[14]

Comparisons of suffragettes and suffragists to women not directly involved in the fight for women's suffrage rely on the commonality between them in order to present the suffragettes, and thus their cause, in the best possible light. Therefore, it is not surprising that comparisons of Englishwomen to women of other nations follow the same lines of nationalist rhetoric that other fashionable discourse does throughout the nineteenth century. As is typical of such comparisons, Englishwomen are described as more beautiful, more discreet, and more tasteful than their French counterparts. In an April 29, 1910 issue of *Votes for Women*, Nita offers in her column "The World We Live In" some "Practical Notes on Present Fashion" that argue for the shifting trends in fashion that offer more choice to the female consumer. Luckily, Nita argues, "London has not yet adopted some of the extremes which have been exhibited in Paris, the Englishwoman showing her customary discretion in selecting new ideas without lending herself to their exaggeration" (497). Like the writers of fashionable texts who employ nationalist rhetoric before her, Nita expresses the belief that Englishwomen are modest and moderate in their fashions; most importantly, however, she expresses this belief in the context of propaganda associated with and published by a militant suffrage group. While some of the viewing public may consider the methods and means of the militant suffragettes also extreme or exaggerated, her call for moderation and restraint in a propagandistic newspaper attempts to disassociate the suffragettes from such considerations. By prefacing this comparison of Frenchwomen and Englishwomen with her use of the inclusive, unifying plural of the first person "we," she thus includes herself and all readers of *Votes for Women*, militant suffragettes, in the designation Englishwomen. This association with the Englishwoman is another means of folding the suffragettes and their cause into the greater fabric of the nation; their cause and their methods should be legitimate because they are Englishwomen.[15]

As the portrayal of the suffragettes and suffragists in fashionable clothing scripts their femininity and unity with women not part of the suffrage movement, the portrayal of the suffragettes in traditional national garb embodies the nation on a synecdochical level. For large-scale events such as the June 17, 1911 Women's Coronation Procession, suffragettes from Ireland, Scotland, Wales, and India wore national dress unique to their country of origin in the British Empire.[16] This recognized and accepted national dress worn to protests and demonstrations became a means of communicating women's rightful place in the construction, maintenance, and promotion of nation. To have a national dress should be to have an important and viable role within the nation itself, as to be representative of the nation should be coupled with representation *in* the nation. Wearing their national clothing, these women argued that to be a good Englishwoman, or a good Irish, Scottish, or Indian woman, was to also be a good British woman and a good British citizen. As for the purposes of protest, Britishness often was conflated with Englishness as in England for the English suffragettes, the two became representative of the each other.[17] Their protests and demonstrations argued that to be a good citizen of their nation, they must have equal access to the rights afforded to the male citizens within that nation. This equality called for a broader role in nation and empire, beyond mere symbolic resonance. This move away from high fashions popular with a large portion of their middle-class contemporaries to national dress rarely worn but instantly recognized establishes commonality with their contemporaries on a symbolic level.[18] The common images of the suffragettes and suffragists show a dual purpose: feminine fashions work in harmony with nationalist symbols, as women and nation are and should thus be considered equally harmonious.

Figure 4.2. Imperial Pageant, Women's Coronation Procession. *Source:* Courtesy of the London Museum. Used with permission.

The suffragettes' use of the national dress unique to their country of origin showed what was present at the demonstrations, a nation's women, but also, what was absent, a nation's men. A nation usually has national dress for both men and women; for suffragettes to protest in national dress without their male counterparts, then, was to argue against the hypocrisy and inequality evident in the construction and governance of the nation itself. While women were allowed to be symbolic representations of the nation, they only were allowed to be symbolic; they could not have the representation that an equal part in the nation would allow. The image of suffragettes in national dress should call forth the image of both sexes standing side by side in complementary outfits. If men and women are meant to represent through their dress the symbolic resonances of nation, then they should have equal access to the practical aspects of nation such as the vote, as well. The Indian suffragettes at the Coronation Procession wear traditional dress recognized as unique to their country of origin; while foreign and exotic to an English audience, their saris are still British by imperial right. While there are men in the background of the picture who seem to be from various parts of the British Empire, none of them wear national dress common to any of the nations of the empire. It does not matter whether the men are there in support of women's enfranchisement or out of curiosity about the procession; by virtue of their sex, they still are recognizable as national citizens. The women alone must rely on national garb to claim the same.

Further, the use of national dress in large-scale demonstrations such as the 1911 Women's Coronation Procession allowed instant recognition of national origin. The coronation demonstrates how often the suffragettes used dress in general, and national dress specifically, to promote their cause among and offer immediate connection to the public. While perhaps not every person may understand the symbolic resonance of the "purple, white, and green" without Pethick Lawrence's written explanation, as in the program for the 1909 Women's Exhibition (13–14), most if not all members of the viewing audience would recognize Scottish, Irish, Welsh, Indian, and even English national dress without benefit of the program. This instant recognition, particularly as it is presented in large-scale demonstrations such as the coronation, serves as a visual language with which to claim and to communicate citizenship. In the Imperial Pageant of the Women's Coronation Procession, "The approach of the Car emblematical of the greatness and unity of the British Empire is heralded by the Union Jack," the program tells us, and followed by "women Pipers in highland dress" to represent Scotland (5).[19] Wales is represented by the Ladies' Royal Welsh Choir, "all dressed in picturesque national costumes," many of which were "old treasured costumes . . . sent from Wales" (5), while Ireland is "heralded by the green flag headed by Pipers in national dress" and "several women from Dublin, wearing 'colleen bawn' cloaks in emerald green" (5). The descriptive language in this program serves both as a helpful description of the processional order and as a reminder of the existence of national dress within the British Empire. The fact that the Welsh contingent wears "treasured costumes" specifically sent to them from their nation of origin and that the WSPU chose to include that information in the program itself is a gentle reminder of women's participation in the building and construction of both their nations and the empire at large prior to the suffrage movement.[20] Rather than presenting women asking for something they do not deserve, these demonstrations in national costumes present women asking for something they should, by consequence of birth, already have.

In an image dated 1909, four suffragettes stand together in recognizable national dress. From left to right, the women are dressed to represent Scotland, Wales, Ireland, and England, the four countries in the United Kingdom.

Figure 4.3. Group of Suffragettes in the Costume of England, Scotland, Ireland, and Wales. *Source:* Courtesy of the London Museum. Used with permission.[21]

Dress alone makes the Scottish, Welsh, and Irish women immediately recognizable, even one hundred years later. The Scottish woman wears a tartan kilt, with knee-high stockings, a feathered bonnet, and a military-style jacket. Both the bonnet and kilt are instant signifiers of Scottishness, as the Welsh woman's hat an instant signifier of Welshness. The difference here, however, is that the Scottish dress is recognizable on both men and women, as the kilt is worn by both genders. Wearing the kilt as national dress, the Scottish suffragette asserts the gender parity her clothing has but that she herself does not. For the Welsh, however, the stovepipe-style hat is the article of clothing that is most recognized as symbolic of the nation, and it is unique to women.[22] Wearing the stovepipe-style hat immediately designated the suffragette as Welsh; wearing the stovepipe-style hat at the Coronation Procession protest immediately highlighted the further hypocrisy of gender inequality in her nation. While her garb is representative of her nation and, specifically, her nation's women, her nation still does not afford her the political representation of the vote. The Irish and the English women's dress, however, are perhaps more subtle indicators of nationality. If the Englishwoman's wide-brimmed bonnet, shirtwaist, and long black skirt do not mark her as English, then the Union Jack slung over her shoulder certainly does: only she has the privilege to wear the flag of empire. The Union Jack also emphasizes the importance of England in the construction of empire and further highlights the conflation of empire with Englishness, rather than the Britishness that would include nations outside of England. The Irishwoman, on the other hand, wears a provincial top, tied in the front, with an apron to denote her more rustic origins. But it is the shawl, knotted at her throat and thrown over her shoulders, that confirms her nationality. Most remarkable about this image is the fact that national identity is defined through dress, and it is defined positively. What the suffragettes accomplish with their call for the spectacle of national dress is to remind their audience that even so-called feminine weaknesses such as clothing have positive and necessary places within the construction and maintenance of nation.

National dress placed the suffragettes within the realm of recognizable British citizens; by wearing the dress visually and culturally associated with their nations of origin, the suffragettes became the "good" British women that writers such as Linton, Ellis, and later even *Votes for Women* columnist Nita cry for. In truth, there is little discussion surrounding the suffrage movement that is not charged with nationalist intention, and we must consider the possibility that most of the suffragettes' and suffragists' attention to dress was put forth with the purpose of gaining the vote.

The larger fight for women's rights, however, encompasses issues other than women's suffrage. Those issues, about the reform of women's dress, about the freedom to move within public spaces, and about the redefinition of women in the popular media, all utilize language and strategies similar to each other in order to vocalize the importance of and necessity for women's active role in nation. Through overt public display like the spectacles orchestrated by the women's suffrage societies, dress becomes socially recognizable as a means of political and national communication.

This is not to say that British suffragettes were the only protesting women interested in the political ramifications of fashion and good dress. Margaret Mary Finnegan's work about American suffragettes, *Selling Suffrage: Consumer Culture and Votes for Women*, argues that "from the movement's beginning, suffragists expressed their demands in material fashion. Whether disrupting civic celebrations or wearing yellow badges, suffragists gave tangible form to their beliefs" (8). What distinguishes these American suffragists from their British, particularly English, sisters, is the influence the British women had on the early twentieth century. As Britain was the seat of imperial power, the array of suffragettes protesting from nations across the globe, including India, Australia, and Canada, as well as the United Kingdom, represented a conglomerate of feminine power over the image presented of both the militant and nonmilitant suffragettes. Tickner reminds us that "the first women's rights convention in the world was held in New York State (at Seneca Falls) in 1848," but even so, throughout the fight for the vote, England remained centrally important to the cause (266). It is for this reason that an examination of British suffragettes over their American or European counterparts, particularly an examination of their iconic clothes and protest movements, is instrumental in determining the importance of a fashionable self to a political cause.

The Personal Is National:
Fictional Suffragettes and Their Fashions

The Edwardian audience encountered the suffragettes not only in newspapers, visual imagery campaigns, and public protests and spectacles, but also in their fictional portrayals in novels. *Ann Veronica*, H. G. Wells's 1909 novel, is particularly concerned with the suffragette's plight and presents a heroine who, like her real-life feminist contemporaries, dresses fashionably, carefully, and well. By looking specifically at a so-called woman's concern like fashion, Wells portrays the difficulties faced by the woman who is interested in social and political change. Further, Wells's novel eschews the still-prevailing Victorian notion of separate gendered spheres by inflating the concerns of the private to the public; the political activism of the suffragettes is as inseparable from the home as it is from the street. When her father and his male friend reminisce that Ann Veronica used to be "all hair and legs" and "Now she's all hat and ideas" (Wells 22), they immediately connect her fashions—that private, personal affair displayed socially and publicly—with her feminist politics, the recent public exhibition beginning to reach new audiences. Their inability to distinguish between Ann Veronica's "hat" and her "ideas" directly references England's larger conflation of a woman's fashion and her political and national affiliations. It also demonstrates how suffragettes leveraged this conflation and even manipulated it to gain equal status as citizens.

Ann Veronica, a motherless young woman living at home with her father, longs for the freedom to attend the college of her choice, to study biology, and to have latchkey privileges. At first, she seems to be all that England fears for its burgeoning suffragette movement. Wells, however, uses the absurdity of some fashions and the acceptable modesty of others to present a heroine who would be both familiar and sympathetic to a potentially hostile audience. He presents his heroine in simple, modest clothing that is always clean and tidy to best present an Englishwoman who is, despite her politics, always embodying the best ideals of her nation; rarely is Ann Veronica seen acting in a manner unbecoming a woman of her class, nation, or age. While she may not wear the Union Jack over her shoulder, her simple, neat dress marks her as a trusted Englishwoman, especially as compared to other suffragettes within the novel. Ann Veronica meets a radical suffragette named Miss Miniver who is "a slender lady of thirty or so" wearing "a dingy green dress" with "an ivory button, bearing the words 'Votes for Women'" on its lapel (Wells 30). The more radical feminists in the novel are identified as shabby harridans who cannot financially afford to be fashionable because of their quest for independence and who are hindered by the desire to express their political views on their bodies. Miss Miniver's dress is both dingy and green, one-third of the common color campaign of the WSPU, and her lapel pin is a political button. Alone, the color green would be insignificant; coupled with the "Votes for Women" lapel pin, the color of her dress signals her political affiliations. Wells takes great pains to separate women like Miss Miniver from women like Ann Veronica, and throughout the novel, "dingy" and "dirty" dress signals more radical and excessively political (i.e., not national) women. Later in the novel, when Ann Veronica meets up with Miss Miniver again, she finds her with "a wild light in her eye, and her straight hair was out demonstrating and suffragetting upon some independent notions of its own" (Wells 109). For Wells, a woman's unkemptness and wildness directly correlates with her political anger; Miss Miniver's "suffragetting" hair suggests that the suffragette's body is out of control. Unlike her real-life counterparts, Miss Miniver does not see the benefits of fashionable and neat dress despite the fact that, like her real-life counterparts, she is angry over her nation's refusal to give Englishwomen the vote.

Miss Miniver's quest to convince the English voting public that she is deserving of the vote is ultimately unsuccessful because she does not pay attention to her dress, whereas Ann Veronica, in her pretty, neat clothes, provides evidence that the suffragettes' conscious use of fashionable middle-class dress has been successful. Ann Veronica "was never awkward, had steady eyes, and an almost invariable neatness and dignity in her clothes" (Wells 39). She, unlike Miss Miniver, respects herself enough to dress with "neatness and dignity" and has the family connections to do so justifiably. When Ann Veronica first leaves home and looks for lodging in London, she understands the dangers a single woman faces in the city, but further, she understands the dangers a single woman may represent to more reputable establishments. Luckily, however, Ann Veronica "was dressed as English girls do dress for town, without either coquetry or harshness, her collarless blouse confessed with a pretty neck, her eyes were bright and steady and her dark hair waved loosely and graciously over her ears" (Wells 80). This simple outfit represents an ideal of English womanhood to which Ann Veronica's class, breeding, and father's financial status allow her access. She knows enough to present a neat appearance and to "[straighten] her hat" (Wells 81) before she attempts to gain lodging at a middle-class hotel. Given the novel's desire to pair hats and ideas, the reader can only assume, and rightly so, that Ann Veronica's ideas will not be far behind.

It is only when Ann Veronica decides that she will participate in a *militant* protest and go to prison for the vote that her politics and her appearance coincide with Wells's conception of the angry, unkempt suffragette—the antithesis of good Englishness. Thus, the novel seems to lose some sympathy for its heroine. As Ann Veronica is pulled away from the steps of Parliament, "Her hair got loose, her hat came over one eye and she had no arm free to replace it" (Wells 192). Like Miss Miniver's, Ann Veronica's hair is also suffragetting. Ann Veronica's youth and prettiness work to garner the reader's sympathy; as Ann Veronica is "clasped about the waist from behind and lifted from the ground" (Wells 192), she is no longer in control of her own body and its movements. Once bodily handled by the police, she can no longer tame her hair as it protests feminine beauty standards for the Edwardian middle class. In fact, Ann Veronica's entire experience of militant protest and arrest frees her body from her command and allows it to protest independently of Ann Veronica. Ultimately, the novel does not see her lack of bodily control as her fault but, rather, the fault of the government that would physically restrain her and incarcerate her.

This image of Ann Veronica is quite similar to images reproduced as postcards and sold to financially support the WSPU, as youth and beauty, as well as good English or national dress, were also used to symbolically represent the suffragettes' political and national cause.[23]

Figure 4.4. A Lancashire Lass in Clogs and Shawl Being "Escorted" Through Palace Yard. *Source:* Courtesy of the London Museum. Used with permission.

Suffragettes utilized the youth and beauty within their organizations to offer a more palpable and desirable public face of their revolution, once again manipulating public understanding of the suffragettes with outward markers such as clothing, fashion, and beauty. The Lancashire lass's simple blouse, shawl, and clogs identify her immediately as a mill worker from the north.[24] As she is not working while she is protesting, the dress functions as a masquerade to present a specific image to the public. Without her clogs and shawl, she is just a young, working-class woman. With them, she is "A Lancashire Lass in Clogs & Shawl," not just a mere "Lancashire lass." In case the viewer was unaware of any significance the lass's seemingly innocuous clothing might have, the text on the postcard happily supplies the information. More than her youth, the identification of her clothing in both image and text calls particular attention to the plight of women like her. This image suggests that she suffers greatly for her lack of vote. Her torn skirt implies her vulnerability, and the two policemen looming over her give every suggestion of the oppression of working women, and even of the sexual threat men may represent to working women. Her skirt is torn high, near her waist, and if she had not been wearing proper undergarments, a signal of her innocence and modesty, her abdomen and pubis might have been exposed. Her loose hair goes even further to mark the physical struggle suffragettes endure to acquire the vote, but one would never say her hair is "demonstrating" or "suffragetting." But the most important signal is her ability to retain her own sense of modesty and national identity. Despite her torn skirt and the violence perpetrated against her, she has through all her struggles retained her shawl. This particular item of dress marks her as an Englishwoman from Lancashire, suggests her employment as a mill worker, and highlights her understanding of the modesty and protection a shawl can afford. Her clothing, identified regionally through the description accompanying the photograph, not only is English but is also specific to the northern region of England associated with industry and manufacture.[25] This identification evokes sympathy for the Lancashire lass from all viewers, even those potentially hostile to the suffrage movement and to the more militant methods employed by the WSPU—not because she is a suffragette but because she is an Englishwoman.

While in prison, Ann Veronica composes a series of couplets that she addresses to her would-be lover, Capes, in which she identifies what she views to be the common symbol for feminine oppression: fashion. Her hallucinatory state prompts her to imagine Capes with her and even causes her to envision him "in a policeman's uniform and quite impassive" (198). Picturing Capes in a uniform symbolic not only of masculine legal power but also of the masculine brute force that carried her off to Canongate, Ann Veronica makes Capes symbolic of institutionalized masculine power. By virtue of his name, Capes is already reminiscent of fashion, and his position as personal protector and symbolic patriarch is here embodied in this poem. In her poem, she emphasizes the vast dichotomies between men's and women's fashions and between men's and women's standards of beauty, particularly highlighted by this uniformed image of Capes. Further, Ann Veronica pays particular attention to the language of clothes and, ultimately, the freedom of movement and freedom of sexuality men's fashions are privileged in possessing.

> A man can kick, his skirts don't tear;
> A man scores always, everywhere.
> His dress for no man lays a snare;
> A man scores always, everywhere. . . .
> For hats that fail and hats that flare;
> Toppers their universal wear;
> A man scores always, everywhere.
> Men's waists are neither here nor there;
> A man scores always, everywhere.
> A man can manage, without hair;
> A man scores always, everywhere. (199)

While some critics have used this poem's simplistic rhyming structure and songlike quality to criticize Wells's commitment to Ann Veronica's feminism, criticism based solely on the poetry's simplistic quality dismisses too quickly the rather extraordinary critique of political change the poem represents.[26] By arguing for the differences between men and women predominantly through the language of clothing, this poem argues for the way in which women's fashion conveys personal and political messages. Because of the freedom of movement trousers allow, "A man can kick, his skirts don't tear"; in contrast to freedom of movement is the suggestion of the artifice of women's dress. It traps and binds not only women but also men; a woman's dress ensnares, but a man's dress "for no man lays a snare." Even the preposterousness of beauty standards for women are called into question, as "Men's waists are neither here nor there" and "A man can manage without hair." Given the propensity of hair to demonstrate and "suffragette" on the women in this novel, the implication is that a man can manage quite well and perhaps succeed even more if he does not have the concerns that his hair will become unkempt and convey a negative social meaning to those viewing him. Even the repetition of "A man scores always, everywhere" suggests the freedom that men have to succeed in life, regardless of situation or circumstance.

At the greatly contested close of the novel, a pregnant Ann Veronica and her now-husband Mr. Capes are welcomed back into the fold of the Stanley family. In both ideals and in appearance, both characters have changed since the start of the novel. Capes's physical appearance has changed little "except for a new quality of smartness in the cut of his clothes" (283), but Ann Veronica's physical appearance is completely different, even to her height. She is "half an inch taller; her face was at once stronger and softer, her neck firmer and rounder, and her carriage definitely more womanly than it had been in the days of her rebellion" (282). Her dress is described in great detail and is quite possibly instrumental in regaining her father's regard (286). When Mr. Stanley asks to have a look at Ann Veronica, he "stand[s] up with a sudden geniality and rub[s] his hands together" (286). Her appearance evokes a physical response in her father, and the "sudden geniality" and act of rubbing "his hands together" is an almost sexual response. She has achieved approval from her father, here representative of a traditional proud English patriarch, and she has elicited a physical sensation from a man, here responsive with the tactile movement of rubbing his hands together. Ann Veronica responds by according him the respect she did not earlier in the novel, as a father and as a man. In response to his reaction, "Ann Veronica, who knew her dress became her, dropped a curtsey to her father's regard" (286). Gone, however, are the sly political insinuations and overtly political fashion statements that saturate the rest of the novel. Ann Veronica has challenged her nation's social and political restraints, and she has not caused its destruction in the process. In fact, her challenges have restored her to England's ideal; as the two wayward lovers are welcomed back into the fold of respectable middle-class society, they do so in contemporary fashionable clothes that convey the good taste that, by virtue of the class to which they were born, they have naturally.

Ann Veronica's fall does not result in the "dingy" clothes so common to the other fallen or outrageous women in the text; rather she "was dressed in a simple evening gown of soft creamy silk, with a yoke of dark old embroidery that enhanced the gentle gravity of her style" (283).

Ann Veronica's designation as a pure and good woman is reiterated by her "simple" clothing and her serious nature. On the one hand, she has resumed the more conservative life assumed proper and traditional for her gender. On the other hand, the nation has not collapsed because of her so-called sexual indiscretion. She has triumphed in love and triumphed in self by returning, celebrated, to the family she "disgraced." Ann Veronica succeeds in living the majority of the life of which she dreamed, leaving possibility open for a return to science and her place in it. The suffragette's connection to both fashion and nationalism is argued most specifically through her struggle to define her place in a nation and society that wishes to contain her. Wells's novel, along with various writings in support of the feminists of England in the late nineteenth and early twentieth centuries, presents an argument that a woman's freedom is not independent of her femininity and that femininity, representative of the best of Englishwomen to England itself, is not independent of a woman's stronger presence in the workings of the nation. Ann Veronica's militant and nonmilitant actions are best expressed through her larger connections to the realm of women's fashion and the struggle to redefine what femininity means.

While Wells's presentation of some of the militant suffragettes is so laughable as to be only deemed caricature, the larger ideas of an English-woman's freedom—of education, of movement, of finance—are staunchly supported throughout the text.[27] A later declaration by Ann Veronica's aunt argues that while suffragettes are "dreadful women," some of them are still "quite pretty and well dressed" (Wells 209). Miss Stanley's exclamation means that campaigns of fashionable and national dress called for by the WSPU are succeeding. National dress placed the suffragettes within the realm of recognizable British citizens; by wearing the dress visually and culturally associated with their nations of origin, the suffragettes are identifiable as the British women that the nation desired. Through overt public display such as the spectacles orchestrated by the women's suffrage societies, dress becomes socially recognizable as a means of political and national communication.

Shopwindow Symbolism:
The 1912 Suffragette Attack on the West End

On March 1, 1912, at 5:45 p.m., members of the WSPU, who had organized in secret, launched bricks, hammers, and stones at dozens of shopwindows in London's popular West End shopping district.[28] Both the time of day (the busy half an hour before the shops closed for the evening) and the places (several of the most popular shops and department stores, including Swan and Edgar's and Liberty's) were carefully chosen to best protest women's lack of vote.[29] The subsequent issue of *Votes for Women* quotes a press description of the event that focuses on the correlation between the militant suffragettes and their supposed purpose in the West End: "Suddenly women who had a moment before appeared to be on peaceful shopping exhibitions produced from bags or muffs, hammers, stones and sticks, and began an attack upon the nearest windows" (352). The clear connection between women and "peaceful shopping exhibitions" is destroyed at the moment politics and fashion violently collide. These seemingly peaceful women retrieve their weapons from innocuous articles of shopping and clothing: their muffs or their purses or shopping bags.[30] Erika Rappaport notes that the gender and class of the women, demonstrated through their clothing, made it difficult for police to tell the difference between militant suffragettes and their nonmilitant shopping counterparts (216). The attack against the fashionable shopping district and against the shopwindows of popular stores, even stores heretofore considered suffragette friendly, was thus considered an attack against the association of women with so-called trivial concerns like fashion.[31]

What is striking about the attack on the shopwindows of London's West End shopping district is not just the militant action engineered to call attention to the suffragettes' cause but also the personalized violence against the fashionable shops that the suffragettes demonstrated. While the suffragettes used the implications of good fashion to help add social respectability to their cause, this attack suggests the anger these women felt over having to appear fashionable, neat, and tidy in order to further their cause. This internalized anger seems to boil over at this moment as it is directed outward at what the suffragettes view to be the very symbol of both their freedom and their oppression. While fashion became an arena through which the suffragettes used and manipulated traditional images and expectations for femininity, it also became a prison in which the suffragettes must constantly exist. Fashion and dress were useful tools in the suffrage movement, but the constant criticisms over unfashionable suffragettes forced them to utilize fashion all the time. Attacking the heart of commercialization and retail, the West End shopping district, and attacking it in the heart of its nation, London, the suffragettes attacked all that the shopping district and the nation represented. Throughout the nineteenth and the beginning of the twentieth centuries, England figured its domestic strength and superiority through its modest and beautiful women, its successful manufacturing industry, and innovation. On March 1, 1912, the suffragettes attacked the nation's conceptions of itself by attacking it en masse disguised as "peaceful" shoppers.

In her unpublished autobiography, actress and suffragette Kitty Marion[32] describes the actions of the 1912 attack as a moment of collusion and understanding between women. As she nears her "scene of action, the Silversmiths' Association and Sainsbury's," a bit earlier than the intended time of attack, she "look[s] round for an encouraging, friendly fellow in the fray" (213). She finally finds "'one of us' a couple of shops ahead, gazing round furtively as I had done. Our eyes met in silent encouragement" (214). Arriving at the shops alone and still finding a friendly face and, later, more fellow suffragettes in the crowd, Marion engages in a communal act with other women at the venues where the communal act of shopping takes place. Marion and her fellow suffragettes appropriate an arena England stereotypically associated with women and vanity and associate it instead with women and militant protest. As the women relied on stereotypes of femininity and women's approaches to the entire fashion system, they manipulated that fashion system to promote the voice that as of yet their nation denied them. They thus turned the destruction of institutions of fashion into vehicles of nationalist discontent.

Yet the fact that suffragettes and suffragists alike, new women, dress reformers, and other feminists used and manipulated popular fashions lessens the immediate and convenient symbolism of such an attack. There is no doubt that the places of attack were chosen specifically for their symbolic resonance as palaces of consumerism most associated with women. So, too, is there no doubt that the busyness of the time of day and the specificity of the place, the most fashionable shopping district in London, ensured that the suffragettes would earn record numbers of eyewitness accounts and press reports. Later issues of *Votes for Women* still utilized department store monies to fund their publications; the March 15, 1912, issue, for example, presents advertisements for Whiteley's spring fashion show (380). While the issue of *Votes for Women* immediately following the West End attack does not list Whiteley's as one of the department stores damaged by the shopwindow attacks (353), it is nonetheless a department store representative of the large-scale shopping center against which the suffragettes protested. Despite their anger against the dependence on fashion forced on them by the society they wish to support their cause, the suffragettes were perhaps even angrier that they were financially dependent on the stores where they had to buy their fashions just to fund the printed vehicle of their cause. Suffragettes, suffragists, and new women activists remained committed to the spectacle of their struggle, and the vast use of images in the expanding field of the popular press ensured that visual imagery was essential in creating a unified and clearly articulated front for the cause of women's suffrage. The fight for the vote and for what the vote represents—women's freedom, independence, and solid position within the nation of England—concerned all of these women. Fashion and dress had viable and important roles in the maintenance of nation, the conveyance of femininity, and the transmission of those beliefs most important to late nineteenth- and early twentieth-century England. These women used fashion in order to best demonstrate their sincere belief that they could embody both their beliefs and England's, both freedom and femininity, both strength and honor and that all of these are complementary rather than mutually exclusive.

Conclusion

To Have and to Wear:
National Distinctions of Dress in Royal Weddings

In March 2020, the world was gripped by the hands of COVID-19. In early March, we had no idea how bad it would get or how many millions of lives would be lost. I was on sabbatical that spring semester, and I had a trip to England planned for research for this very chapter. I didn't find out until the night before I was supposed to leave that our university president approved my leaving on university business, because at the time, the United Kingdom wasn't at high risk for COVID.

Of course, COVID spread very quickly, and I was only one week into my two and a half week stay in the United Kingdom and Ireland when the US Department of State called American citizens home. Ireland closed its borders, letting no tourists in and only letting them out. I had one day to decide to get home, and that was only if I was *allowed* to leave. Talk of shutting down airports was happening in louder and louder whispers, and I had friends trying to help me find housing in the United Kingdom if for some reason I was trapped.

No one knew what COVID would do to the world, not at that time. There were no vaccinations, just death tolls, racing upward, and I confess that my mind wasn't quite on research that final day in the archives. I had just settled my new flight the day before, getting home a week and a half before I was supposed to. The heroes in the university's travel office—surely, you have similar heroes in your university or place of business—found a flight home for me, and I was leaving Saturday morning. I tell you this because the research I did that last day at the Fashion Museum in Bath, one of my absolute favorite archives to visit, was rushed by the fact that

I had to get back to London and pack for a very early trip to Heathrow the next morning.

But I had my train ticket to Bath, and I had an appointment at the Fashion Museum that I had made several months before. The only thing I would do in London that day would be to pack and panic, so I decided to go ahead with my research visit, if for no other reason than that I now had no idea when I would ever be able to get back to England for research. The Fashion Museum's collection manager, Fleur Johnson, pulled several wedding dresses for me, spanning early nineteenth century to the late 1800s, and, Reader, they were all beautiful. Some lace and silk, some with matching shoes and gloves, many were from my favorite era of fashion, the 1880s, when the bustle reached its height of popularity. So I was surprised that when I fell in love with a gown that day, it was from 1851.

This gown was one of the last I was presented with, Fleur bringing it out for two reasons: one, because it was pink, even with the fashion for white gowns after Queen Victoria's wedding in 1840 (most of the gowns I saw that day were white), and, two, because it was made and purchased right there in Bath at Jolly's Department Store. This dress, it seemed, had a story to tell. Not always do archives get provenances with the clothing, and not only did we know where it was made and sold, we also knew about the woman who wore it.[1]

Sometimes we forget that these dresses had real people inside of them. To remind myself, I often look inside the dresses or for patches on shawls for those signs of wear and tear that are common with consuming fashion. This pink dress from Jolly's was well-preserved, still with fringe along the sleeves and neckline. But there was also dirt preserved at the bottom of the dress and on its underside, the smudged material that so fascinated me because it proves that it was worn, and loved, and preserved as it was.

Further, knowing the provenance of this particular dress was readily available meant that the conclusion I had been researching, this as of yet elusive wedding dress chapter, would come full circle. This pink wedding dress was a dress that represented England. It was made in England, sold in England, and specifically regional to Bath, and Jolly's was still an operating department store (after I left the archives, I had a quick tea at Jolly's before catching an earlier train back to London). I was able to walk where that dress had been, evidenced by the provenance cards with it, and see perhaps what Mrs. Thomas Radford Hope had seen. Different materials and goods in the department store, certainly, but the building was the same. It made me wonder about Mrs. Thomas Radford Hope and her choice of a pink wedding dress. Was it her favorite color? Did she choose it because of her spring (May 15, 1851) wedding? Unfortunately, the museum does not have the original communication about the dress (although the provenance card says letters exist), so we are only left to speculate as to this special dress, unique during a time of white wedding dresses and orange blossom accessories.

When I was thinking of an appropriate ending to this book, I kept coming back to Queen Victoria, again and again. For my own wedding, I wore white not because I look good in white—I rather don't like it, generally, as a color on me—but because in 1840, Queen Victoria wore a white dress with orange blossoms and a fashion for white wedding dresses became all the rage.[2] Before that, women wore their best dress, possibly their Sunday best, or a special dress for the occasion.[3] Some may have been white, certainly, but the queen brought along the craze for it, the fashion for it, a long-lasting legacy well into the twenty-first century.[4]

Royal wedding dresses, more than wedding dresses for the rest of us, are symbolic in ways beyond white virginal expectations. In looking at royal wedding dresses, we see not only yards of white satin or silk and lace and tulle but also representations of items important to the bride in the way of embroidery or important to the nation in terms of place of construction (e.g., Queen Victoria's Honiton lace). Queen Victoria herself had coded messages in her ensemble, and this continued for Queen Elizabeth II, as well as the recently wedded royals: Eugenie, Kate, and Meghan.

For this conclusion, I'd like us to look together at royal wedding dresses, to look at the sartorial messages of brides from Queen Victoria to the more recent brides of Buckingham Palace, because ultimately, what these dresses prove is that fashion and nationalism are still inextricably entwined. We will see this especially in the dress of Meghan Markle, who used symbols both of her American background and her husband's British background in her embroidery, melding the two countries together in one beautiful gown.

Queen Victoria

Weddings are all about spectacle, are they not? Fancy dresses and tuxedos or suits, flowers, an elaborate cake (or cupcakes, or donuts, for the trendy bride), weddings are made not just for the symbolic passing of bride to groom or bride to bride or groom to groom, but also for the entertainment of the masses. I say "masses" as someone who invited 625 people to my own wedding (my mother knew just about everyone in New Orleans) but also in thinking about royal weddings. Royal weddings, like Victoria's, were publicized in great detail for everyone in England to partake in the event. You may not get a slice of cake, but you get to see what the cake looked like and imagine how it tasted. But while scholarship on wedding cakes and the royal wedding exist, in my research I found none that tied the royal weddings of the last two centuries together, specifically looking at the gowns. I saw this gap in scholarship and decided to close it.

Speaking of cake, great work has been done on wedding cakes and spectacle, most particularly the wedding cakes of the royal family of England. Emily Allen's "Culinary Exhibition: Victorian Wedding Cakes and Royal Spectacle" speaks of Queen Victoria's wedding through the lens of the public images of the wedding cake. She writes, "When Queen Victoria staged her marriage as a massive public spectacle, neither the condition of England nor the condition of her crowds was perfectly stable" (463). Allen chooses her words carefully here: staged, public, spectacle, because that is what we see with royal weddings and, indeed, most modern weddings as well.[5] My own wedding took place on the same day as a popular football game in New Orleans, and tourists wandered in off the street and joined the crowd to watch us get married—literally, the public viewing something that was not necessarily private but shared among family and friends. But then, when I left my parents' house to go to the church, the entire neighborhood came out and watched as I and my bridesmaids walked to the cars waiting to take us away. Spectacle, it seems, is an important component of weddings, whether the bride wants it to be or not.

Of course, Victoria wanted her wedding to be a spectacle, because of the unrest beginning in the 1840s, the Hungry Forties as they came to be known, but also the German background of her Albert needed to be erased. Allen reminds us that with the marriage, Albert is considered an English subject (464) and that "the royal wedding cake bore no trace of Albert's German pedigree, but instead Classicized the couple—appealing to a shared Roman ancestry, which flattered Britain's imperial fantasies" (464). Victoria and Albert must represent a united English front, against any encroaching foreignness. Elizabeth Langland, in "Nation and Nationality: Queen Victoria in the Developing Narrative of Englishness," argues that "In Victoria, a national idea finds its articulation through gender, race, class, and ethnicity. As woman, mother, wife, and widow, empress of India, and queen of England, Victoria becomes a site for the concept's simultaneous consolidation and contradiction" (112). Both symbol of nation and nation itself, Victoria was in a unique position to declare herself a maiden bride through her choice of dress and flowers. She becomes England: pure, untainted, exploratory. One way that a young Queen Victoria accomplishes this is through her careful dressing and planning of her wedding.[6]

I unfortunately could not get access to the royal wedding gowns during my trips to England; when I inquired with the Royal Collection Trust, I was told that the contemporary gowns (those of Eugenie, Kate, and Meghan, etc.) were in private ownership, while the older gowns (those of Queen Victoria and Queen Elizabeth II) were displayed publicly. I understood of course. It was a rather American question, after all. I wanted to touch these gowns, feel the laces, chosen specifically and purposefully to represent England, and the best of England at that.

So to the internet and popular texts we turn. According to the Royal Collection Trust's website, Queen Victoria's gown was made of Honiton lace, which the website claims the commission of "reviv[ed] the flagging lace industry of Honiton, Devon." Choosing this particular lace from this particular place is a very queenly thing to do. To commission part of a wedding dress from a specific area of England, and an area that needed money, is an action that leads a country in no small way. The website also tells us that "In further support of English industry, her dress was made of East London (Spitalfields) silk." Another purposeful move to show her leadership of the country, but also her faith in her people. Queen Victoria did not go to Paris for her dress; she stayed home and chose to honor materials made by her people for her, specifically, and we learn from the website that it was probably made by Mary Bettans, a longtime dressmaker for the queen.[7] Nigel Arch and Joanne Marschner's work *Royal Wedding Dresses* for the Historical Royal Palaces, note that:

> It was of concern to Queen Victoria and her advisers that the entire bridal outfit should comprise materials of British manufacture. Accordingly, the silk satin was obtained from Spitalfields, in London. Mrs. Bettans, the Queen's dressmaker, had the task of making the dress, which was eventually trimmed with a spectacular set of English Honiton lace made under the supervision of Miss Jane Bidney, "lace manufacturer in ordinary to the Queen." Miss Bidney returned to her native village of Beer in Devon in order to better undertake her commission, employing more than 200 workers between March and November 1839. (10)

Further details on an additional page at the Royal Collection Trust inform us that the nation critiqued Victoria's "preference for French textiles," as represented by the remark by Lord Melbourne. We cannot deny that France was a center of the fashion industry, certainly, but to assume that France is the *only* center of the fashion industry is to deny the designers and makers of England and America, who were doing excellent, beautiful work, important work, haute couture work, and that English and American fashions are equally beautiful and as important as their French counterparts.

The Fashion History Timeline on the FITNYC (Fashion Institute of Technology in New York City) website specifically mentions that the dress is made of all English materials, noting that because the nation's industries were in decline, Victoria specifically chose domestic materials for her gown. The website describes the gown as follows: "The structured, eight-piece bodice features a wide, open neckline. The off-the-shoulder sleeves are short and puffed. The pointed waistline is deep v-shaped, resembling the basque shape. Both the neckline and sleeves were trimmed with lace. The floor-length skirt was very full, containing seven widths of fabric in forward-facing pleats. At her wedding ceremony, Victoria wore a satin train over six yards long, which twelve attendants carried down the aisle." The dress is at the height of fashion for the end of the 1830s (my least favorite era of fashion, to be honest), but the dress itself is lovely and doesn't swamp the diminutive queen. But what is also important about her dress is the detail that went into it. That lace, so beautiful, made from a flagging industry, decorated the gown with *English* materials. Later royal brides go even further in representing England in their looks, as we shall see with Queen Elizabeth II.

Queen Elizabeth II

Helen Bradley Foster and Donald Clay Johnson's "Introduction" to *Wedding Dress Across Cultures* discusses the importance of dress in general and the wedding dress in particular. They argue that "Perhaps the most visible and telling of dress modes are wedding garments, the choice of which makes a statement by showing comparative prestige, wealth or perceived status. Part of cultural tradition, it changes only in modest increments. In a larger sense, wedding dress forms a complex set of interlocking relationships that tie a society together as it unites a couple in marriage" (1). In this estimation, nation and society can be seen as interchangeable when considering royal weddings. For Queen Elizabeth II's wedding, although at the time she was Princess Elizabeth, it was a time of austerity. England was still recovering from World War II, the Blitz, and rationing of food and cloth affected the people throughout the country.[8] Kimberly Chrisman-Campbell tells us that in the time post-WWII, "Clothing rationing hit brides particularly hard. When Princess Elizabeth announced her engagement to Philip Mountbatten in 1947, people across the country sent her their coupons for her wedding dress. She returned them all, using her own (plus two hundred gifted by the British government) to purchase her satin and lace Normal Hartnell gown" (135). But what ties Elizabeth's dress to our argument about nationalism and fashion are the tiny mementos of nationalist pride we see. In her book *HRH: So Many Thoughts on Royal Style*, Elizabeth Holmes notes, "Elizabeth requested symbols of the United Kingdom and Commonwealth countries—including the Canadian maple leaf, New Zealand fern, and Pakistani wheat—to be portrayed in sumptuous silver, gold, and pastel embroidery on her white satin gown" (19). For a beautifully fictionalized and well-researched detailing of Elizabeth's dress, I recommend Jennifer Robson's *The Gown: A Novel of the Royal Wedding*, which was meticulously researched and describes nearly every detail of the gown that the princess wore, all encompassed in a very compelling plot to protect the dress from the adamant press. But as we look at historical sources, we see that Elizabeth wanted to represent her country, her empire (flagging though it was), in the symbolic representations of her dress. Using Chinese silkworms and English designers, and adding symbols of England, Canada, New Zealand, and Pakistan on her dress drives home for this future queen that she will be queen of a vast empire rather than a single country.

Further, these symbolic gestures are just that: symbolic gestures that reach out to the viewer and convince them that Elizabeth cares for her empire, cares enough for its people to represent them in her very personal wedding dress. She was not queen yet, so she did not wear state robes, but Victoria started the craze for white wedding dresses specifically by choosing *not* to wear her coronation robes. She wanted a "simple" dress, a descriptor that belies the yards of lace and silk, but these royals are, at their core, women who want to look pretty in a pretty dress. Perhaps, like me, Elizabeth and Victoria chose dresses that they wore, rather than dresses that wore them.

The Brides of Royalty:
Kate, Eugenie, and Meghan

Not since Diana's wedding to Prince Charles has England seen such an outpouring of interest in the royal family. The scandal of Charles and Camilla, the tragic death of Diana, the suffering of her two sons, all have been weathered it seems to arrive at these moments: the royal weddings of Harry and William to Meghan and Kate, respectively. Of course, like their royal predecessors, Kate's and Meghan's dresses had meaning beyond simply "marriage." Elizabeth Holmes writes of the general clothing of the royals, not least of which are their wedding dresses, and notes of the recent royal brides, "Their wardrobes are a treasure trove of meaning. . . . If this is one way these women speak, then this is one way we should listen" (8).

This statement appeals to me as a fitting end to this work. Clothing speaks, and it is one way women communicate. And if this is the way women communicate? We *should* listen. There is something they have to say. What better time to communicate than a highly publicized royal wedding? Kate, Meghan, and Eugenie all communicate with their wedding gowns, from their choice of designers and materials to the symbolic embroidery on veils or in lace, to the very endearing and provocative open back of Eugenie's dress, showing off her scoliosis scar from surgery.[9] We have been spoken to; it is our job to listen.

Meghan Markle is perhaps the most fascinating of the recent royal brides, especially since she and Harry have chosen to leave royal life. But before they did, there was a royal wedding to take place. Meghan wore a dress that Elizabeth Holmes calls "stunning in its simplicity" (249). Holmes later tells us that "The drama of the design, and the burden of tradition, was placed entirely on the sixteen-foot veil. Embroidered with each of the Commonwealth countries' flowers, it was held in place by Queen Mary's diamond bandeau tiara on loan from Queen Elizabeth II" (249). To further add to the representation of the items on her veil from the Commonwealth, there are "two special, personal additions: winter sweet, which grew near Meghan and Harry's cottage on the grounds of Kensington Palace, and the California poppy, the flower of the bride's home state" (274).

Kimberly Chrisman-Campbell informs us about Kate Middleton that she "and Alexander McQueen designer Sarah Burton looked to previous royal brides—notably Princess Grace and Princess Margaret—for inspiration for the gown . . . the bodice and skirt appliquéd with Carrickmacross lace handmade at the Royal School of Needlework" (34). Not only was Kate's choice of Sarah Burton from Alexander McQueen a representation of English manufacture—especially given the tragic suicide of McQueen before the commission—but the lace itself is representative of Great Britain and its former empire, as the lace's patterns originate in Ireland, and were handmade, specifically for Kate, at the Royal School of Needlework.[10]

These women, knowing their very personal weddings would be public spectacles, chose their dresses and their creation and materials carefully to communicate the strength of England and the strength of these women, Kate and Meghan not aristocrats themselves, to navigate the rather treacherous waters of the British paparazzi, which, as we know from Diana's tragic death, can be brutal and fatal.

Conclusions to Conclusions

In June 2021, a very unique and unexpected opportunity fell in my lap to teach at Harlaxton College for the July term during a pandemic. The original instructor unfortunately had to back out because of a family emergency, and ten days before the term was scheduled to start, I applied, and was hired, to teach British Literature to American students in Harlaxton, England.

Reader, it was a whirlwind of course, trying to get the appropriate paperwork finished and plane tickets ordered and quarantine supplies shipped (we had to take COVID tests at designated points during quarantine), but I arrived at the end of June and spent ten days in quarantine with a wonderful group of students, faculty, and staff. At the end of our ten days, we took all the students to London for a weekend of experiential learning. Among other interesting dilemmas, it was the Euros final in London, and London was swarming with people.

One of my students expressed a wish to see Princess Diana's wedding dress on display at Kensington Palace, and it grew into, as she said, "a whole thing." Suddenly, from three to four students and me going, it swelled into over twenty people, faculty, students, and staff alike. We took the tube, got separated, found each other again, and hiked our tired feet through the park to end up at the palace.

I separated myself from the group for a number of reasons: one, I prefer to enjoy museums at my own pace, as I like to linger, or not linger, on my own schedule. But also, I was ecstatic because this was, at last, the natural conclusion to the conclusion of my book: Princess Diana's wedding dress. I wanted to experience it on my own, look at it with my own eyes, and not concern myself with lecturing to students about the fashions (as, let's face it, I'm wont to do).

You have to walk through the entirety of Kensington Palace before you can go to the Orangery, which is where Diana's dress was housed. I confess I sped a little through Queen Victoria's childhood home, so eager was I to see the dress display. But soon I was done and walking through the garden to get to the Orangery. There was an entire display on royal fashions, but the only wedding dress on display was Diana's.

It was stunning.

The dress itself is very iconic 1980s, of course, with its gigot sleeves and flared skirt. But what makes it extraordinary are two things: its color and its train. Diana was not married in bright white but instead was married in ivory, a decision made to compliment her skin tones. And her train, which was twenty-five feet long, was displayed in the Orangery behind the glass, stretched out in all its glorious detail.

I wish I could say I took the perfect picture for you. I wish I could show you what I saw, how I saw it (with tears in my eyes, of course, not only because it was Diana's dress, but because it was so perfect for my book). Unfortunately, I am a terrible photographer, and my pictures show reflections in the glass, other people crowded around, and terrible lighting and angles. So I just put my phone away and experienced it.

We often forget that we experience fashion. We don't just wear it; we enjoy it; we appreciate it; we want new things or old things (as I write this, '90s fashion has come back into play and I have seen some granny dresses like I wore in the 1990s and of course, my Doc Marten boots are now the height of couture). Fashion is, as I hope this book has proved to you, a lived experience. And part of that lived experience is nationalism.

Sadly, there were few details on the display about Diana's dress. So I bought the exhibit book to bring home and use for my research then went to the café and got the first proper coffee I had had since I arrived in England and sat and thought about the dress. About Diana. About Kate and Megan. About Victoria. About what it means to both *be* a symbol of a country and *wear* a symbol of that country. Was I so obviously American in my dress? Of course in my accent, but was my desire to see royal wedding dresses, and Diana's in particular, an American experience? Are Americans interested in the royals because we don't have them or because everyone has always been interested in the royals?

I have no answers for you other than this: royal wedding dresses articulate nationalism in a bold and persuasive language that is easily decoded and understood. Nineteenth-century women, however, articulated nationalism through more subtle means—by eschewing the crinoline (or wearing it), by wearing the corset (or rejecting it)—and women continue to speak nationalism today, by declaring something "good" and "English" in the same breath as one speaks of strawberries. Nationalism, and displays of nationalism, are about pride but also about ownership and place. I am a part of my nation, these fashions say, despite your attempts to remove me. I am a good English woman despite your lack of trust and respect. I am worthy, of respect, of the vote, of a voice and place within the nation in which I reside. Not at all frivolous, fashion has played an important and, indeed, vital role throughout history but, during the nineteenth century, came to mean so much more than just clothing one places on a body.

It says, I am England. These words, thanks to fashion, are no longer merely symbolic but spoken with the voice and agency denied of women for so long.

Notes

Introduction

1. I am in no small part indebted to the work of Nancy Armstrong. Upon first reading her work *Desire and Domestic Fiction: A Political History of the Novel*, I was challenged to rethink my own notions regarding the public and private spheres of nineteenth-century women's lives. Armstrong argues that there is a "relationship between the sexual and the political" and that "political events cannot be understood apart from women's history, from the history of women's literature, or from changing representations of the household" (10). Dress is an intimate part of women's history and of the household; I argue that it is also an intimate part of women's involvement with their nation.

2. In *Seeing Through Clothes*, Anne Hollander challenges the common understanding of the naked body as the natural body in her claim that the clothed body is just as natural, as people spend most of their time dressed rather than undressed (84).

3. For further information on the function of women's magazines in the nineteenth century, see Jeffrey A. Auerbach's "What They Read: Mid-Nineteenth Century English Women's Magazines and the Emergence of a Consumer Culture" and Margaret Beetham's *A Magazine of Her Own? Domesticity and Desire in the Woman's Magazine, 1800–1914*. Also, *Victorian Women's Magazines: An Anthology* edited by Margaret Beetham and Kay Boardman offers an overview of the various types of women's magazines available in the nineteenth century.

4. In *National Identities and Travel in Victorian Britain*, Marjorie Morgan argues that "When touring the Continent, travellers from Britain typically deferred to this tendency to lump all people from the British Isles together as 'English.' Robert Louis Stevenson, for example, wrote at length about his Scottishness when in America, but nearly always identified himself as an 'Englishman' if talking with Europeans" (195). We can see a similar sentiment in England, as well, particularly when identifying all peoples from the British Isles as "English" is helpful in furthering a cause, like the women's suffrage movement.

5. In her article on Mary Seacole's *Wonderful Adventures of Mrs. Seacole in Many Lands*, Poon discusses Englishness and its "irreducibly *performative* nature as discourse" (501, emphasis original).

6. My understanding of nation and nationalism is further indebted to Benedict Anderson's *Imagined Communities: Reflections on the Origin and Spread of Nationalism* and Linda Colley's article "Britishness and Otherness: An Argument."

7. Colley in *Britons* argues that "it was during this period that a sense of British national identity was forged, and that the manner in which it was forged has shaped the quality of this particular sense of nationhood and belonging ever since" (1).

8. Patrick Parrinder's *Nation and Novel: The English Novel from Its Origins to the Present Day* offers an interesting discussion of what makes English novels particularly English, from the eighteenth century to the twentieth, and argues that "it is not merely coincidental that the English novel rose to prominence in the eighteenth century when Britain was fast becoming the centre of a world empire" (2). Parrinder in part sees literature in constant dialogue with empire.

9. In *Britons*, Colley remarks on a parade in celebration of peace in 1814 England for which men and women dressed up as the Duke of Wellington and Britannia, John Bull and Mrs. Bull (237). Colley argues that parading Mrs. Bull "side by side with her 'husband,' John Bull, suggested that the claims of women were coming to be recognised in this society in a new way. By participating as actors and not just as spectators in this victory procession . . . women proclaimed that they, too, were patriots who could make an active contribution to the nation's welfare and progress" (237–38). Interestingly, "Mrs. Bull" is a woman identified as patriotic, not only through her participation in the parade but also through her symbolic costume. While this celebration early in the century helps to establish women's participation in nation, I argue that it is in their everyday dress and, most particularly, in their use of fashionable dress rather than their use of costume that allows women agency in their participation in nation and establishment of their nationalism for England. This use of costume, however, will become very useful for the suffragettes and suffragists at the end of the century.

10. There are several texts that have been extraordinarily helpful in establishing my understanding of women and nation and women and empire. Deirdre David's *Rule Britannia: Women, Empire, and Victorian Writing* examines writing about nation within the larger British empire and, in particular, "within this writing the nation about women, women themselves, of course, participated in its construction: sometimes in enthusiastic consonance with praise of Britannic rule, sometimes in a contrapuntal voice that speaks skeptically alongside the primarily androcentric voices that articulate ideal governance of the empire" (5). Bernard Porter's *The Absent-Minded Imperialists: Empire, Society and Culture in Britain* understands that "nineteenth- and early twentieth-century British imperialism was not only 'masculine' in character, but also included some conventionally 'feminine'

traits" but as these traits existed "without any input at all from the women, so far as we can judge" (292), those traits are more ideological constructions of gendered conventions. Susan Meyer's work *Imperialism at Home: Race and Victorian Women's Fiction* explores how Victorian women writers used the language of race as a way to access larger discussions of gender (7). Anne McClintock seems to summarize the overall experience of gender and nationalism quite nicely by arguing that "All nationalisms are gendered, all are invented and all are dangerous" (352).

11. Alison Goodrum, in her discussion of the English Burberry check, still sees this importance as late as 2001, when she argued that "The ideas of national identity that are reproduced and represented through the images of iconic clothing organizations are fundamentally connected to ideas of gender, race, and sexuality" (89) and that "This repetition and ritualistic commodification of a gendered national identity manufactures and manifests not only a national 'us,' but also a national 'them'" (91).

12. For further discussion of wearing ribbons as alignment with politics, albeit in the earlier Restoration, see Edward Legon's "Bound Up with Meaning: The Politics and Memory of Ribbon Wearing in Restoration England and Scotland."

13. Kristin Hoganson's "The Fashionable World: Imagined Communities of Dress" looks at class and nationalism and their roles in the fashionable arena. She argues, "The key to the appeal of French fashions lies in the imagined community it implied, and this community stretched across national boundaries, uniting upper-crust consumers" (265).

14. Ada S. Ballin in *The Science of Dress in Theory and Practice* (1885) even sees tight lacing along a national divide, noting, "Although French ladies wear as tight corsets as their English sisters in folly, they do not suffer so much from their effects, and this for a good reason. English ladies pride themselves on being 'always fit to be seen,' and they therefore wear their corsets all day long, and remove them only when they go to bed. French women, on the other hand, have certain times at which they are 'on view'; when they ride in the Bois or visit, and for evening wear they lace as tightly as the English; but when they are in their own houses and not going to receive, stays are thrown aside, and their tortured bodies are allowed to expand to their natural proportions. Hence with them the evil is confined to a few hours in the twenty-four, whereas with the English it extends to fourteen or more, and the harm done is correspondingly greater" (161).

15. Georg Simmel in "Fashion" (1957) discusses how the lower classes imitate the fashions of the upper classes (556). Fanny Douglas in 1895 would also agree with this model, because "As a rule, the society woman drops a mode as soon as the suburban belle discovers it, and the suburban discards it as soon as 'Arriet lays hold of it" (7). And Sarah Stickney Ellis in *The Daughters of England* (1842) asks, "Shall we continue to compete with our servants in dress, now that excess has become an evil; or shall we endeavour, for their sakes as well as our own, to compete with them in self-denial, and in courage to do right?" (166). The

nineteenth century is rife with manuals on how to prevent servants from dressing like their employers, and these concerns span the Victorian period, as evidenced by Ellis's 1840s concerns that reach out to Fanny Douglas's fin de siècle concerns.

16. Crane notes that after the 1960s, the bottom-up model of fashion occurs, with clothes coming from the lower classes (14).

17. In the same way that I've been asked how my male students feel about my "playing with fashion," I have also been asked how my husband responds to my fashionable leanings. Reader, I can assure you that my husband is both aware of the difference between a crinoline and a bustle and aware of the fact that women dress for other women. As my writing partner, he has absorbed a lot of fashionable writing over the years.

18. Fred Davis notes that historical record and recent scholarship both insist that fashion is strictly about "sex appeal" (81). Further, Davis discusses the theory of the shifting erogenous zone attributed to J. C. Flugel although there is no evidence it is actually something the psychologist wrote (83). The theory proposes that fashion emphasizes or hides particular aspects of women's bodies in order to draw attention to them (82–83). Such actions could include the flappers of the 1920s rouging their knees, which were suddenly visible after centuries of being hidden. Davis agrees that sex is not the only thing fashion is concerned with (81).

19. Festa notes, "That English women may alter their complexion at will in conformity to custom suggests the malleability of French and English alike. Although English adherence to the French fashion *ought* to suggest that all women are equally artificial, the journalist in *The Connoisseur* invites nation to trump sex. The natural truth of Englishness is sustained despite the feminine submission to French fashion: the 'genuine glow of a British cheek' is discernible from and superior to the 'false faces' of the Parisian ladies, with their 'faint lustre of *French* Paste'" (32).

20. Hazen Hahn reads nineteenth-century French fashion magazines and notes that the idea that Paris was the "capital of fashion at the time" is communicated through both English and French magazines (220). The article argues that "English fashion magazines of the period by and large derived, or copied, their fashion plates from French magazines" (220).

21. Lori Anne Loeb argues that advertisers wanted to reach women at home because women were the "power of [the] purse in household affairs" (8).

Chapter One

1. Terri Hasseler remarks that "Crinolines were often extremely dangerous, catching fire and severely injuring their wearers; they were cumbersome and made getting in and out of doorways and carriages difficult, sitting down became a laborious process, knocking objects off shelves was a natural course of

events, and bending over was often indecent" (129). While some of these stories of dangerous crinolines were hyperbole, enough reports in the press made it appear more than hearsay.

2. Diana C. Archibald's *Domesticity, Imperialism, and Emigration in the Victorian Novel* argues for the dual definition of "home": "Home is not a physical space alone but a combination of house and feeling (i.e., home is constructed not merely of brick and mortar but, more important, of 'Peace' and 'love'). Home is 'a sacred place,' made so by the efforts of its inhabitants, particularly the women. . . . Indeed, not only does woman create the domestic space, but that space also helps create her" (6). Ellis would certainly support this argument, as her tracts involve the concerns of women within both the physical and the symbolic space of "home."

3. *The Women of England* is succeeded by tracts addressed to daughters, mothers, and wives.

4. I define *national dress* here as clothing that is racially, culturally, or socially constructed to represent and distinguish visually one nation's citizens from those of another.

5. Julie Fenwick's "Mothers of Empire in Elizabeth Gaskell's *Cranford*" argues that "the majority of middle-class male characters who do appear in *Cranford* are involved in such military imperialism" as is concerned with activities "that serve to keep the domestic mills of Drumble supplied with raw materials and foreign markets" (410). Fenwick draws a direct connection between military/imperialism and the availability of textiles and therefore a direct connection between military/ imperialism and the creation of fashion.

6. Mary insists, "If we wore prints, instead of summer silks, it was because we preferred a washing material; and so on, till we blinded ourselves to the vulgar fact, that we were, all of us, people of very moderate means" (4). Here, too, Mary's suggestion that the Amazons actively choose to be unfashionable argues for Cranford's contrariness.

7. Roze Hentschell notes that in the sixteenth and seventeenth centuries, foreign textiles "represented leisure, decadence, disease, and—most crucially—dissolution of the virtues associated with English textiles, such as charity, hospitality, and humility" (545).

8. For further information about the English manufacture of foreign fabrics, "Spinning Cotton" and "Kashmir Shawls in Mid-Victorian Novels" by Suzanne Daly and "The Kashmir Shawl" by Sarah Buie offer insight into the birth of the shawl trade in Paisley, Scotland, and other parts of Great Britain. John Irwin's *The Kashmir Shawl* also gives an excellent history of the Kashmir shawl itself.

9. Suzanne Daly in "Kashmir Shawls in Mid-Victorian Novels" notes that "They are also a coveted gift that men returning from colonial service in India bestow upon their mothers and sisters" (238), and that in "most English novels, we only see shawls once they enter the realm of the domestic, where they are offered up to women as gifts" (248).

10. Nupur Chaudhuri's "Shawls, Jewelry, Curry, and Rice in Victorian Britain" notes that "Genuine Kashmir shawls were expensive, costing between seventy and one hundred pounds each in the 1810s. Since the cost of an Indian shawl was so high, its market was limited to wealthy women" (233).

11. Daly and other critics differentiate between the Kashmir shawl, which refers to shawls made specifically in Kashmir, and the more generic Indian shawl, which refers to shawls made in varying parts of India. For the purposes of this article, the Kashmir and Indian shawls will be treated interchangeably, as it is their symbolism that is important for this work; once in Gaskell's version of England, both types of shawls mean the same thing, despite their manufacture.

12. Chaudhuri notes, "Its aesthetic value aside, the Kashmir shawl was also considered to be an item of tangible wealth. The shawl from India was listed in *trousseaux*, and the item was regarded as a valued inheritance" (234).

13. At one point in the text, Mary recounts the pretensions of the milliner's shop, which forced those "without a pedigree" to go rather to "the universal shop, where the profits of brown soap and moist sugar enabled the proprietor to go straight to (Paris, he said, until he found his customers too patriotic and John Bullish to wear what the Mounseers wore) London" (60–61). Here, the origins of dress and fabric are literally and figuratively being rewritten as English for the benefit of the patrons.

14. Later in the century, Mary Eliza Haweis's *The Art of Dress* (1879) discusses the transmission of fashion from Parisian designers to English milliners and how designs change to cater to English sensibilities. For Haweis, this carries disastrous results: "The ordinary milliner gets a pattern dress or bonnet from some firm in Paris which has copied some Parisian *élégante*, who may possibly possess an eye for colour. The *élégante* invents a combination; the trade-houses catch it up more or less exactly; they transmit it to England, and generally the second and third editions show signs of having suffered a decided change" (114–15).

15. Mary Brooks Picken's *A Dictionary of Costume and Fashion, Historic and Modern* tells us that corded means the petticoat would be "ribbed as if with cords or cord-like stripes or lines, as cloth having lengthwise ribs produced by warp; crosswise, by weft; diagonal, by twill weave" (81). The corded petticoat would be a stiffer garment, and would help the skirts of the dress bell out becomingly. This will of course be supplanted by the very cage crinoline Mary speaks of.

16. Mary Brooks Picken's *A Dictionary of Costume and Fashion* notes that "in England," calico is "plain white cotton cloth. So called for Calicut, India, where cotton textiles were first printed" (43). The cage is thus transnational: a French fashion trend, using Indian fabrics, gaining popularity in England.

17. While Victorian fashion tracts are rife with concern over servants' superior knowledge in the arena of fashion, this story's addition of a man to that mix seems unique. However, Mr. Hoggins's position as town doctor gives him access to the particulars of the female form, which Miss Pole does not believe gives him "a right to be indecent" (178). Gaskell avoids a direct suggestion of indecency by

giving the authority to Mr. Hoggins's wife, who enjoys fashion books so much that Mr. Hoggins "can't help seeing the plates of fashions sometimes" (178).

18. Mary Brooks Picken's *A Dictionary of Costume and Fashion* tells us that a calash is a "Hood made on hoops" (42) "to be pulled over head or folded back. Fashionable in 18th century, after introduction by Duchess of Bedford. Copied from folding hood or top of calash or light carriage" (176).

19. Christina Lupton's "Theorizing Surfaces and Depths: Gaskell's *Cranford*," argues for the importance of materiality in this scene in "The Cage at Cranford" and states, "Taken as a key to *Cranford*, this episode underscores how thinking about text as fabric, not metaphorically but materially, gives Gaskell the opportunity to gesture to local practices of meaning making without condescension, legitimating the various ways in which her text secures its futurity in the living rooms and train stations of the future" (250).

20. Karin J. Bohleke's 2010 article, "Americanizing French Fashion Plates: Godey's and Peterson's Cultural and Socio-Economic Translation of *Les Modes Parisiennes*" examines the history behind the copying and altering of French fashion plates for an American audience, noting that such examination "reveals a complex cultural and economic negotiation between French and American society and fashion cultures of the mid-nineteenth century (1850–1865)" (122). Her acknowledgment of the complexity of these negotiations helps to challenge assumptions regarding the national origins of nineteenth-century fashions.

21. While these transformations may seem confined to working-class or economically poorer women who could not afford to purchase the latest fashions new, it is counterintuitive to assume that only poor women altered their fashions. In fact, many fashion trends are sparked by personal alterations, desires, or requests. MacDonald et al.'s *Whistler, Women, and Fashion* tells us that "Worth introduced looped-up crinolines with ankle-length skirts, revealing colored stockings and walking boots" in 1863, at the request of Empress Eugenie (26).

Chapter Two

1. Dress reform happened throughout the nineteenth century, with concerns about corsets, crinolines, and bustles, as well as trains on dresses dragging detritus from the street into the home. Several sources, including *Punch*, mock the dress reform movement as ugly fashions for unattractive women.

2. A description of the corset on the London Museum website is as follows:

This corset was designed by Madame Roxey Ann Caplin, a staymaker of Berners Street, London. It is believed to have been shown at the Great Exhibition in Hyde Park in 1851, where Caplin was awarded a prize medla [*sic*] of "Manufacturer, Designer and Inventor."

Roxey Ann Caplin and her husband invented and patented many corsets and corset "improvements" between 1838 and 1860. This corset is noticeably light-weight, as the designers reduced the amount of boning and removed the large busk (metal support) from the centre front. Caplin described herself as an inventor rather than a dressmaker.

She also published a book in 1864, titled "Health and beauty: or, woman and her clothing." In this book she defended the corset against men who did not understand the comfort, support and protection they provided. But she believed that corsets could be better designed to suit women's bodies, and that as a woman, she was better qualified to make them.

When this corset entered the London Museum collection in 1937, it was descibed [*sic*] as follows:

Has the special openers called "Dr Caplin's busks" after the patentee of the process. These stays were exhibited at the Great Exhibition by the firm of Madam Caplin, and the stand won the only bronze medal given for this type of work. The color is merely . . . for exhibition purposes. Nothing but white, grey or black corsets being made for the respectable public. The buttons on the side of the strap are intended for the petticoats and the hook went over the front of the petticoat to prevent it from riding up and bunching around the waist. (London Museum, *"Description." Roxey Ann Caplin Corset*)

3. Nancy Marck Cantwell argues that corsets remain important to both men and women in Thackeray's novel, noting that corsetry becomes "a means of imposing a national identity based on self-control, a uniform that could supersede differences of race, gender, and social class, and which is the subject of considerable resistance in Thackeray's novel" (par. 1). Men's uniforms are particularly important in Thackeray's novel but not for our purposes here, as this book focuses on women's clothing rather than men's. For excellent discussions of men's clothing in the nineteenth century, consult Brent Shannon's *The Cut of His Coat*, John Harvey's *Men in Black*, and Anne Hollander's *Sex and Suits*. For discussions of uniforms as items of men's clothing, see work by Jennifer Craik.

4. This essay was a chapter in *Crossings in Text and Textile* edited by Katherine Joslin and Daneen Wardrop, University of New Hampshire Press, 2015.

5. While Becky is only half-French, the English in the novel read her as entirely French and therefore a conniver.

6. Interestingly, Cree LeFavour's chapter "Acting 'Natural': *Vanity Fair* and the Unmasking of Anglo-American Sentiment" tells us that for American audiences,

Becky Sharp was seen as natural. LeFavour also notes, "To be 'natural,' then, had a dual and somewhat contradictory meaning since it simultaneously signaled effortless, authentic performance of the 'self' while also indicating an undesirable absence of cultivation and domestication most damningly and shockingly linked to female sexual passion which in turn is coded black" (par. 42). Taking LeFavour's argument into consideration, we can see that unlike English readers who understood 'natural' to be both authentic and a representation of English nationalism, American audiences read "natural" as racially rather than nationally charged.

7. Dobson writes, "While Rebecca's identity is often viewed explicitly as a performance, Amelia's 'appropriately' feminine and English identity, consciously or not, remains a naturalized performance—it is simply performed with far greater success" (2). Other critics argue similarly to Dobson in reading Amelia's behavior as performative. In "Female Sexuality and Triangular Desire in *Vanity Fair* and *The Mill on the Floss*," Phyllis Susan Dee reminds us that "if gender is performative . . . , Amelia's submission, self-effacing behavior may conceal a more complex personality" (392). It is my argument, however, that while gender and femininity are important constructs to Victorian womanhood and are well discussed in *Vanity Fair* criticism, we must not lose sight that fashion, dress, and style were intricate parts of women's lives in the nineteenth century, as they are today. Ultimately, these concerns are writ, first and last, in the fashionable arena.

8. Mary Hammond notes that "Becky's flattery and falsehoods are intolerable precisely because they are in danger of professionalizing—and therefore exposing to the world—the performances by which other women secure their futures. Intolerable, too, is her genuine Frenchness. Not the gentile [*sic*] Frenchness of the aristocracy, but the common, dangerous Frenchness which threatens middle England" (33).

9. Earlier in the novel, all of Becky's clothes come to her secondhand, either as Amelia's castoffs or as gifts from admirers bought at secondhand shops or auctions. One example that contradicts this theory would be Becky's presentation at court, for which she robs the Crawleys' ancestral wardrobes, picking through old dresses to secure quality brocade and lace (Thackeray 558). Here, older clothes offer Becky respectability and authenticity because they give her the illusion of an English pedigree.

10. In "Siren and Artist: Contradiction in Thackeray's Aesthetic Ideal," Judith Law Fisher reads this scene as demonstrating "Becky's mechanical skill at arranging her portrait . . . emphasized by the theatrical lighting and careful composition of the scene" (399). Fisher contrasts what she calls "Becky's manufactured brilliance" (399) with Amelia's "genuine 'pink and white' beauty" (399) and "sincerity" (400).

11. The other women in the novel who possess Becky's power of reading and interpreting fashion are, surprisingly, the Misses Osborne, George's sisters. They often shred Amelia's confidence with their "bold black eyes" because they read through her outward appearances and find them wanting. Or, as the narrator reminds us, "the Misses Osborne were excellent critics of a Cashmere shawl, or a

pink satin slip; and when Miss Turner had hers died [*sic*] purple, and made into a spencer; and when Miss Pickford had her ermine tippet twisted into a muff and trimmings, I warrant you the changes did not escape the two intelligent young women before mentioned" (150). The social power they have, while not vast like Becky's, is, like Becky's, dependent on their fashionable vision.

12. This English belief in a furtive, French knowledge of fashion can be dated as late as the 1890s, as George Meredith's title character from *Diana of the Crossways* is accused of having "the secret of dressing well—in the French style" (140–41).

13. Nancy Marck Cantwell, in "Waist Not, Want Not: The Corseted Body and Empire in *Vanity Fair*," elaborates on other critics' arguments about *Vanity Fair* "by calling attention to corseting as a means of imposing a national identity based on self-control, a uniform that could supersede differences of race, gender, and social class, and which is the subject of considerable resistance in Thackeray's novel" (par. 1). She argues, "From ball gowns to uniforms, dress serves as a public discourse through which national identity is performed and national image formulated and disseminated" (par. 1).

14. I am extremely grateful to Dr. Anne Longmuir at the 2009 Victorian Markets and Marketing Conference for pointing out that Amelia is pregnant in this scene, which allowed me to question further Becky's purpose in reprimanding Amelia's wardrobe choices.

15. Of interest to note is the continuing debate—well into the twenty-first century—regarding the role of the corset in Victorian women's lives. While nineteenth-century women did wear corsets during pregnancy, there was concern over spontaneous miscarriage because of tight lacing. The fact that Amelia's corset seems to fit so poorly suggests that she is, in fact, not participating in tight lacing and is being quite cognizant of the concerns corsetry might present to the health and safety of her unborn child. As always with Amelia, at the moment she is her most natural—especially when considering her physically apparent maternal body—she is her most unsuccessful at being beautiful, despite what the characters in the novel claim. For further discussion on the use of corsets in pregnancy, please consult any of the excellent works by Mel Davies, Valerie Steele, or Leigh Summers.

16. Even Becky's good housewifery is artificial, albeit successful. The narrator tells us that "a good housewife is of necessity a humbug" (211). In this sense, then, Becky performs an acceptable role.

Chapter Three

1. Natalie M. Houston argues:

The history of clothing is particularly useful to Eliot's narrative project because clothing is simultaneously material and symbolic in both text and world. Costume signifies aspects of human personality to readers of literary texts as well as to social observers in the real world. Clothing is also a necessary feature of social existence and is therefore a component of the world which realism attempts to represent. The depiction of clothing in novels thus partakes of the same tension between art and the representation of the actual world as does realist narrative itself. (23)

2. For further readings of Eliot's works and fashion and materiality, see Jean Arnold's "Cameo Appearances: The Discourse of Jewelry in *Middlemarch*"; Kate Flint's "The Materiality of *Middlemarch*"; Clair Hughes's *Dressed in Fiction*; and Andrew H. Miller's *Novels Behind Glass: Commodity Culture and the Victorian Narrative*.

3. In *Dressed in Fiction*, Clair Hughes's research informs us that Eliot conducted extensive research into the clothing for *Romola*, visiting both Italy and the British Museum (90).

4. Clair Hughes argues that "The contrast between Dorothea Brooke and Rosamond Vincy in *Middlemarch*, for example, is often seen as that between a noble woman and a modish coquette. High-minded women, we assume, are not interested in dress, but they play key roles in George Eliot's fiction" (104).

5. Carol-Ann Farkas in "Beauty Is as Beauty Does: Action and Appearance in Brontë and Eliot" notes that "Regardless of what the world may have thought, both Charlotte Brontë and George Eliot considered themselves to be physically unattractive by the standards of the day. Both women, to varying degrees, found their looks to be cause for serious reflection, if not actual anxiety" (324).

6. Royce Mahawatte's chapter "The Sad Fortunes of 'Stylish Things': George Eliot and the Languages of Fashion" acknowledges that "across [Eliot's] fiction-writing career, which spanned over 20 years, Eliot's references to clothes, material culture, hairstyles and fashion cycles more generally, are extensive" (69) yet ultimately argues that it is all part of "Eliot's criticism of fashion" (70).

7. Suzanne Keen in "Quaker Dress, Sexuality, and the Domestication of Reform in the Victorian Novel" discusses the Quakerish dress of both Dorothea Brooke and Jane Eyre and argues that despite what many think of the sexlessness of Quakerish clothing, it would in fact be "a promise of spirited sexuality" (211). Krista Lysack notes that "What is striking about Dorothea's parade of Quakerish, even funerary clothing is the excessive nature of its plainness" (*Come Buy* 101).

8. Clair Hughes says, "Dorothea's self-fashioning, if inconsistent and theatrical, is essentially outward-looking: she wishes to make life, everybody's life, beautiful" (108), which in essence would include Dorothea's life as well.

9. There are several tracts against the dangers of the crinoline available for review in the British Library. My personal favorite, "THE DANGERS OF CRINOLINE, STEEL HOOPS, &C" by an anonymous author, describes women being struck by lightning or falling into water or fires because of their or others' crinolines. Of course, the dedication is to "The Wives, Mothers, and Daughters of the United Kingdom."

10. Even to writers who love fashion, such as Elizabeth Gaskell, fashion can seemingly signal weakness and vanity. *Mary Barton* and *Ruth*, in particular, offer circumstances in which Mary's aunt becomes a prostitute because of her love of dress and Ruth is seduced precisely because she works for a dressmaker and is in constant contact with fashion. But the loving portrayal of both characters belies Gaskell using them as warnings rather than female characters worthy of our sympathy.

11. Kate Flint in "The Materiality of *Middlemarch*," argues that "The society of Middlemarch is bound up with the material in the most literal of senses. The town's economy, like that of its outlying villages, relied heavily on the textile industry—specifically the weaving of silk ribbons" (67). Ribbons are a fascinating part of women's fashion because they hold no use; they are used purely for aesthetic purposes. They are only representative of beauty and fashion.

12. In her article "Inventing Reality: The Ideological Commitments of George Eliot's *Middlemarch*," Elizabeth Langland sees Dorothea's attention to clothing and then her ultimate rejection of it in this scene to be "a mark of Dorothea's innate nobility of spirit" that she is able to dismiss items of clothing like her bonnet and gloves so easily (93). Langland also sees several moments of the text as enacting "the dialectic of nature and artifice" as "an opposition to nobility and commonness," in which "attention to clothing reveals one's commonness" (93). Dorothea's constant attention to clothing throughout the novel, however, belies this belief in "commonness."

13. This is often read much differently, but in *Come Buy, Come Buy*, Krista Lysack argues that *Middlemarch* "produces plainness and understatement as a fetish" (98) and that Dorothea's appearance "is no less an effect of commodity culture for its effort to efface that relation" (98).

14. In the Broadview edition of *Middlemarch*, the footnote to this passage on the "Henrietta-Maria style" states that Charles I's queen often was painted wearing a similar style of necklace (38).

15. Gordon Bigelow in "The Cost of Everything in *Middlemarch*" looks at jewelry in both *Romola* and *Middlemarch* and notes, "In *Romola* (1863) Eliot gave considerable attention to the powers of gemstones and the sometimes outlandish meanings assigned to them in human history. There, as in *Middlemarch*, part of what was implied is a refutation of charges of feminine vanity attached to the ornaments of dress. In showing that the jewels have unique and powerful characteristics in themselves, characteristics that appeal keenly to the senses, the

text rejects the suggestion that their value is simply a concoction of the female imagination, authorized by husbands and fathers via the process Veblen would label vicarious consumption" (98–99).

16. Sally Shuttleworth argues that *Middlemarch* is a novel "fascinated by bodies, and their role in social culture" (425).

17. Jean Arnold's article "Cameo Appearances: The Discourse of Jewelry in *Middlemarch*" offers a thorough and fascinating critique of the use and language of jewelry, not only in Eliot's novel but also in the Victorian age at large. She argues that despite Dorothea's understanding of the jewels as symbols of a political or economic system that counters her aesthetic values, she retains the jewelry because "she will consistently embrace belief systems grounded in aesthetic values" (267). Arnold also sees some jewelry as having "imperial power" in the Victorian age (268).

18. Clair Hughes sees "Dorothea's delight in the gems" as suggesting "an aesthetic need, and a half-conscious sense of how they might enhance her looks" (93). I argue instead that there is little that is "half-conscious" about Dorothea's understanding of how to figure her body and beauty best.

19. Fred Davis understands antifashion as "usually viewed by those in authority in these [strongly authoritarian or totalitarian] societies (as well as by a populace perhaps in sympathy with its manifestation) as a form of political protest. It is thereby automatically rendered suspect" (165–66). While the society of Middlemarch is neither "strongly authoritarian or totalitarian," it still views Dorothea's fashionable choices as different.

20. Hughes understands Dorothea's plain dress, particularly her plain sleeves, as "conspicuously different, an intentional difference, perhaps, to Aesthetic or 'reformed' dress of Eliot's own time. Dorothea's image is neither in nor out of fashion: acceptable to a reader of 1871, it is also comparable to a timeless Bible verse or poem set gravely amid the day's trivia" (93).

21. In his work on men's clothing, *Men in Black*, John Harvey acknowledges:

> In the novels by women, writing on women's dress, that the best light is shed on the real and serious importance of dress: as when, in *North and South*, the true nobility of Margaret Hale, both of her figure and of her spirit, is made visible by a particular dress, or as when Dorothea Brooke in *Middlemarch*, preparing for a difficult interview with the woman she believes to have seduced the man she loves, draws strength from the attention she gives to her toilet. . . . The world of dress, and of talk about dress, is, in the nineteenth century especially, a woman's world. (197)

Harvey uses this understanding of the importance of dress in women's lives to highlight the supposed femininity in importance of dress in men's lives.

22. Andrew H. Miller argues that at the same time "Eliot conventionally genders domestic concerns, linking material culture with mood, habit and women," she is "clearly devaluing feminine material culture—it opposes 'responsible' reason. Her discomfort with material culture arises from the ability, associated with the feminine, to operate beneath the notice of reason" (192). Miller sees Dorothea's fashionable choices as disdainful of feminine interest in dress (192), despite the fact that Dorothea truly enjoys and appreciates clothing.

23. Hughes concludes her statement by noting that it is "playacting mitigated, however, by a desire to submit to some ideal task or person, and inspired by idealism, by 'all that is fine' " (94).

24. Suzanne Keen argues that Quakerish dress in novels like *Middlemarch* and *Jane Eyre* is actually erotically charged and not as Puritanical as standard readings might attest (227).

25. Kate Flint argues that Rosamond "herself is, of course, the novel's most notorious clotheshorse" (69).

26. Lydgate falls into debt partly because of Rosamond's desire for pretty things but also partly because he does not understand money or the amount he himself spends on clothing and items of the house. The text notes that "Lydgate believed himself to be careless about his dress, and he despised a man who calculated the effects of his costume; it seemed to him only a matter of course that he had abundance of fresh garments—such things were naturally ordered in sheaves. It must be remembered that he had never hitherto felt the check of importunate debt, and he walked by habit, not by self-criticism. But the check had come" (466).

27. Hughes argues that right before writing *Middlemarch*, Eliot was chastised by Owen Jones for her inattention to personal dress and that this might have influenced her attention to clothing in the novel (91).

Chapter Four

1. London Museum, "Stockings," accession no. 55.29a–b, permanent collection.

2. Part of this chapter was published in *Critical Studies in Fashion and Beauty*, vol. 3, nos. 1–2 (2012): 55–67.

3. Kimberly Wahl informs us that "For members of the WSPU, white stood for purity, green for hope, and purple for dignity" (21).

4. In "Fashion, Femininity and the Fight for the Vote," Rolley tells us that "while the WSPU was reluctant to give specific written advice on the suffragettes' everyday dress, *Votes for Women* did include a fashion column in sixteen issues from 30 July 1908 to 17 November 1911" (52). This column from Nita is by no means unique in its discussion of fashion and its role in the suffragette's life, and is in fact one of many Nita composed for *Votes for Women*.

5. Lisa Tickner informs us that *suffragette* was a derogatory term first used by the press before it was affectionately reclaimed by the members of the militant WSPU (8). I use *suffragette* rather than *suffragist* because it was the term prevalent during the period between 1909 and 1912, and particularly for the WSPU, on whom this chapter will focus most specifically.

6. Rolley reminds us that "garments and details of appearance were used to signal deviation from or adherence to the feminine ideal" (51). As these early feminists were concerned with public appearance, they wished to signal adherence to that ideal.

7. Katarzyna Kociolek's "London's Suffragettes, *Votes for Women*, and Fashion" reminds us that:

> Notorious depictions of the WSPU (The Women's Social and Political Union) activists as unattractive and badly dressed women, who neglect their womanly duties and poorly perform as mothers or wives, undoubtedly motivated the suffragettes to look smart. Therefore, contrary to the press misrepresentation, clothing and accessories were widely used by Emmeline Pankhurst and her fellow activists to gain visibility and increase public support for the suffrage movement. Pankhurst's elegant and stylish personal appearance as well as deliberate use of clothing and costumes during the protests and marches may be viewed as a direct response to these negative representation of the suffrage movement in the media. (88)

8. London Museum, *"Women's Suffrage Calendar for 1899,"* accession no. 50.82/106, Women's Suffrage Collection.

9. I am focusing specifically on British suffragettes, but the American suffragettes also used spectacle, color, and pageantry to convey their demand for the vote. See Sarah J. Moore, "Making a Spectacle of Suffrage: The National Woman Suffrage Pageant, 1913."

10. "According to one suffrage song of the International Woman Suffrage Alliance, 'Whatever our race or country be . . . we are one nation/Womanhood'" (Burton 173). Antoinette Burton discusses how both the militant and the non-militant branches of the women's suffrage movement tried to unite across creed and nation by declaring them all to be women first and foremost, which we know now was deeply problematic in ignoring the concerns and effects of the empire on women of color.

11. From the Women's Library, London School of Economics, *"Hugh Franklin and Elsie Duval Papers" Collection, Folder 3: Miscellaneous Papers,* 7HFD/A/3, Box #FL226.

12. From the London Museum, *Prison Letters, Police Summons, Prison Records, "Leonora Tyson letter collection from Holloway,"* addressed *"My Dearest Diana" on Sunday March 24, 1912 12:30 p.m.,* Suffragette Collection.

13. From the Women's Library, *Militant Suffragettes, Index 1911–1912, No. 190, Box #6.1, 9/20/105, Box 4 vol. 10–22*, Autograph Letter Collection. The blue skirt she requests is from a letter dated March 16, 1912 and addressed "Dear Ernie."

14. Mary Brooks Picken's *A Dictionary of Costume and Fashion, Historic and Modern*, itself a republication of *The Fashion Dictionary* originally published by Funk &Wagnall's in 1957, is an indispensable resource for identifying specific fabrics.

15. Of course this is problematic, in that women of the empire, however "British," were not "English." While the suffragettes could pretend a conflation of every woman in the empire gave them access to legitimacy, the long history of white women using women of color in protest marches and as symbolic representations to further their own goals and not seeking the same for their women of color counterparts would defy these attempts. I attempt to discuss suffragettes from the empire as representative of fashion and nationalism by the images alone. I leave it to more knowledgeable scholars to further the discussion of the empire on the suffrage movement. For further information, see Antoinette Burton's *Burdens of History: British Feminists, Indian Women, and Imperial Culture, 1865–1915*.

16. From the London Museum's Suffrage Collection, accession number 001489.

17. In America, like England, nationalism was dependent on whiteness, which Philip N. Cohen explains as practicing "a nationalism based on exclusive citizenship that was conditioned on whiteness. I see these politics as national-ist—embedded within the women's experience and conceptions of *America*—as well as 'racist.'" (707).

18. Elizabeth Wilson sees national costume to be a hybrid of peasant dress and fashion: "In many European countries the peasantry continued to dress distinctively. They often aspired to fashion, however, and what is now known as 'national costume' is in many cases a hybrid adaptation of peasant styles to symbolize a newly created national identity when the nineteenth-century nation states were formed. Some of the most seemingly 'authentic' of these costumes may therefore represent the rewriting of history, a kind of sartorial lie" (*Adorned in Dreams* 23). The focus on recreating authenticity is particularly interesting when examining the formation of nation-states in nineteenth-century Europe, as the establishment of national identity is most dependent on spectacle.

19. From the London Museum's archives, *"Memento of Women's Coronation Procession to Demand Votes for Women Order of March and Descriptive Programme,"* 17 June 1911.

20. Lisa Tickner argues that "Symbols must be recognisable if they are to be used in public discourse or they will not carry meaning. What matters is their legibility and not, for the purposes of communication, their 'truth.' Once Welshness was associated with a certain costume, so that association was con-solidated by its use in a new construction of 'women-of-Britain'" (128). Tickner notes the legitimacy of the association of symbolic costume; I, however, argue

more for the role of national dress not only as symbolic spectacle but also as a logical counterpart to wearable articles of fashion.

21. From the London Museum, accession no. 50.82/1307, Women's Suffrage Collection. Unfortunately, there are several copies of this picture in the museum archives, and each has a different date and accession number. I use this particular image for clarity, and the date 1909 because of the date, "April 19, 1909," printed on one of the other copies of this image.

22. Colin McDowell's *Hats: Status, Style, and Glamour* tells us that "throughout the eighteenth century, men and women in Wales wore round-crowned felt hats and it was not until the 1820s that a taller hat began to be worn. The hat now considered part of the national costume was largely the mid-nineteenth-century invention of Augusta Hall, later Lady Llanover, as part of her dual campaign to promote a national costume and encourage the tourist trade" (127). While its purpose was created for women by a woman, its heyday was brief and thus became part of the traditional national costume.

23. The London Museum identifies her as Dora Thewlis, a sixteen-year-old mill girl (https://www.londonmuseum.org.uk/collections/v/object-453455/a-lancashire-lass-in-clogs-shawl-being-escorted-through-palace-yard/).

24. From the London Museum, *Postcards*, accession no. 50.82/1722, Women's Suffrage Collection.

25. Wendy Parkins's "What to Wear to a Protest March: Identity Politics and Fashion in the Suffrage Movement" includes further discussion of the figures of such women and uses the figure of Annie Kenney, another such "Lancashire lass," to argue that "middle-class femininity" was not "the only identity assumed to legitimize suffragette political action" (77). Katrina Rolley points out the importance of the Lancashire lass's class in the effectiveness of image, as "struggle was always absent from WSPU postcards. The factory worker's age and class allowed this depiction—a middle-class woman in the same position would have been unthinkable" (Rolley 53). Also, of course, quite noticeable is her lack of hat, another marker of her working-class status.

26. Anne B. Simpson suggests that "Ann's ruminations on what it means to be a woman in a repressive patriarchy are trivialized by the recurrence of a ditty that she finds herself compulsively composing in her head" (42).

27. Perhaps this laughable presentation is unsurprising, as Maroula Joannou reminds us that "Wells was not opposed to women's suffrage but was deeply hostile to the social purity and anti-male strands within the organized feminist movement" (200). As Miss Miniver is often portrayed as anti-male, her suffragetting hair seems particularly vindictive on the part of Wells.

28. The March 8, 1912 issue of *Votes for Women* summarizes several newspaper reports of the incident ("Some Press Descriptions," 352).

29. For the entire list of shops damaged and the monetary damage incurred, see "Shops That Suffered" in the March 8, 1912 issue of *Votes for Women* (353).

30. Caroline Howlett notes that the language of fashion is significantly changed by concealed weapons such as hammers or bricks and that "Feminine dress could no longer be assumed to denote feminine subservience in its wearer, but on the other hand it could not, of course, be assumed to denote militancy: in other words, by 1913, femininity had lost its stability as a signifier in the heterosexual economy" (77).

31. Parkins sees a parallel between the way the militant suffragettes were dressed and the way the mannequins were dressed to advertise the newest styles. She argues that despite some critics' beliefs that the destruction of these similarly dressed mannequins is symbolically self-destructive, "women's fashionable dress is a sign not of their victimization, but of their empowerment" (80).

32. Marion, *Autobiography*. From the Women's Library, collection, reference no. 7/KMA or 7/YYY6, Box FL639.

Conclusion

1. Batmc I.28.83/5/5b/5c 1851 earliest date. Jolly's of Bath. Silk woven grosgrain.

2. Laurie Essig reminds us that for the color white, "The whiteness was to signify sexual purity, but this sexual purity was never separate from racial purity in England or the United States. Slavery and colonialism were built on the bodies of women, marking some as virginal and others as hypersexualized. The white wedding dress always bore both gender and racial hierarchies" (39).

3. Barbara Penner notes, "Since the wedding of Queen Victoria in 1840, the white wedding had been growing in popularity among fashionable Protestants, but brides from dissenting religious denominations, immigrants, rural inhabitants, and the less-well-to-do still wed in color" (2).

4. Sarah Heaton notes that "It was, however, Queen Victoria's endorsement that fixed the white dress in the cultural consciousness. Her choice of dress suggested her feminine identity rather than her state identity" (84).

5. Also see Adele Wessell's "Having Our Cake and Eating It Too: A Reading of Royal Wedding Cakes."

6. For a detailed analysis of Queen Victoria's wedding lace, which was worn many times after the wedding and loaned to various women in her family for their weddings or their children's christenings, see Kay Staniland and Santina M. Levey's "Queen Victoria's Wedding Dress and Lace."

7. Janice Helland offers the following background to the creation of Queen Victoria's wedding dress:

Queen Victoria's patronage of the industry coincided with an attempt to decrease the reliance upon imported lace and later in the century complemented campaigns to encourage "buying British." By the 1880s "buying British" had become a familiar cry amongst politicians, philanthropists and merchants as they attempted to encourage home production and thwart the ever-increasing demand for imported goods. The Marquess of Salisbury, for example, in a speech made in 1881 in support of the British woollen industry, insisted it was a "matter of national interest that purchasers of textile fabric" give preference to British goods. He also acknowledged fashion as a "great force" that could be wielded by "all women in England" because it determined the "destiny" and influenced the "wealth and poverty" of large sections of the "labouring and industrious population." Lord Salisbury concluded his speech to an audience of over 700 people by suggesting that "ladies of England may be persuaded to prefer goods which give employment to British artisans, British farmers, and British labourers, that they remember there is something more important than the gratification of their own taste." (194)

8. Elizabeth Holmes notes that Elizabeth II's dress: "was made of elaborately embroidered duchesse satin with a fifteen-foot silk tulle full court train. She wore pearls given to her by her father and Queen Mary's Fringe Tiara, on loan from her grandmother for the occasion. With the spectacle came scrutiny, too. Ahead of the wedding, inquiries were made about the origins of the silkworms used in the design (can you even!). The palace confirmed they were from China, rather than Italy or Japan, which had recently been enemy territories" (18).

9. Kimberly Chrisman-Campbell informs us that "Her wedding gown—designed by London-based Peter Pilotto—had a deep V neckline in the back, framing her scar" (35).

10. Elizabeth Holmes writes, "It was a wedding gown for the ages, timeless rather than trendy, with a close-fitting corset-like bodice and padded full skirt reminiscent of Victorian styles. Praise was widespread and effusive, the influence nearly instantaneous. Strapless dresses had been the near-ubiquitous choice for brides, but Kate made sleeves chic. The dress also set a new course for the Alexander McQueen label, boosting the house's commercial future a year after the designer's tragic suicide" (172).

Works Cited

Allen, Emily. "Culinary Exhibition: Victorian Wedding Cakes and Royal Spectacle." *Victorian Studies*, vol. 45, no. 3, Spring 2003, pp. 457–84.

Alter, Peter. *Nationalism.* Translated by Stuart McKinnon-Evans, Edward Arnold, 1985.

Anderson, Benedict. *Imagined Communities: Reflections on the Origin and Spread of Nationalism.* 1991. Verso, 2006.

Arch, Nigel, and Joanne Marschner. *The Royal Wedding Dresses.* Historic Royal Palaces, 1990.

Archibald, Diana C. *Domesticity, Imperialism, and Emigration in the Victorian Novel.* U of Missouri P, 2002.

Armstrong, Nancy. *Desire and Domestic Fiction: A Political History of the Novel.* Oxford UP, 1987.

Arnold, Jean. "Cameo Appearances: The Discourse of Jewelry in *Middlemarch*." *Victorian Literature and Culture*, vol. 30, no. 1, 2002, pp. 265–88.

Atkinson, Diana. *Suffragettes in the Purple, White, and Green: London 1906–1914.* Museum of London, 1992.

Audax, Frederick. *A Hint from Modesty to the Ladies of England on the Fashion of Low-Dressing.* London, F. W. Wheeler, 1855.

Auerbach, Jeffrey. "What They Read: Mid-Nineteenth-Century English Women's Magazines and the Emergence of a Consumer Culture." *Victorian Periodicals Review*, vol. 30, no. 2, Summer 1997, pp. 121–40.

Ballin, Ada S. *The Science of Dress in Theory and Practice.* London, Sampson Low, Marston, Searle, & Rivington, 1885.

Barthes, Roland. *The Fashion System.* Translated by Matthew Ward and Richard Howard. Hill, 1983.

Batchelor, Jennie. "Let Your Apparel Manifest Your Mind: Dress and the Female Body in Eighteenth-Century Literature." *Styling Texts: Dress and Fashion in Literature*, edited by Cynthia Kuhn and Cindy Carlson, Cambria Press, 2007, pp. 113–28.

Beetham, Margaret. *A Magazine of Her Own? Domesticity and Desire in the Woman's Magazine, 1800–1914*. Routledge, 1996.

Beetham, Margaret, and Kay Boardman, editors. *Victorian Women's Magazines: An Anthology*. Manchester UP, 2001.

Bigelow, Gordon. "The Cost of Everything in *Middlemarch*." *Economic Women: Essays on Desire and Dispossession in Nineteenth-Century British Culture*, edited by Lana L. Dalley and Jill Rappoport, The Ohio State UP, 2013, pp. 97–109.

Bohleke, Karin J. "Americanizing French Fashion Plates: *Godey's* and *Peterson's* Cultural and Socio-Economic Translation of *Les Modes Parisiennes*." *American Periodicals: A Journal of History, Criticism, and Bibliography*, vol. 20, no. 2, 2010, pp. 120–55.

Bourdieu, Pierre. *Distinction: A Social Critique of the Judgement of Taste*. Translated by Richard Nice. Harvard UP, 1987.

Bowlby, Rachel. *Carried Away: The Invention of Modern Shopping*. Columbia UP, 2001.

Breward, Christopher. "Femininity and Consumption: The Problem of the Late Nineteenth-Century Fashion Journal." *Journal of Design History*, vol. 7, no. 2, 1994, pp. 71–89.

Buck, Anne M. "Clothes in Fact and Fiction 1825–1865." *Costume: The Journal of the Costume Society*, vol. 17, 1983, pp. 89–104.

Buie, Sarah. "The Kashmir Shawl." *Asian Art and Culture*, vol. 9, no. 2, Spring/Summer 1996, pp. 39–51.

Burton, Antoinette. *Burdens of History: British Feminists, Indian Women, and Imperial Culture, 1865–1915*. U of North Carolina P, 1994.

Cantwell, Nancy Marck. "Waist Not, Want Not: The Corseted Body and Empire in *Vanity Fair*." *Nineteenth-Century Gender Studies*, vol. 11, no. 2, Summer 2015, https://www.ncgsjournal.com/issue112/cantwell.html.

Cass, Jeffrey. " 'The Scraps, Patches, and Rags of Daily Life': Gaskell's Oriental Other and the Conversation of Cranford." *Papers on Language and Literature*, vol. 35, no. 4, Fall 1999, pp. 417–33.

Cavallaro, Dani, and Alexandra Warwick. *Fashioning the Frame: Boundaries, Dress and the Body*. Berg, 1998.

Chalus, Elaine. "Fanning the Flames: Women, Fashion, and Politics." *Women, Popular Culture, and the Eighteenth Century*, edited by Tiffany Potter, U of Toronto P, 2012, pp. 92–112.

Chaudhuri, Nupur. "Shawls, Jewelry, Curry, and Rice in Victorian Britain." *Western Women and Imperialism: Complicity and Resistance*, edited by Nupur Chaudhuri and Margaret Strobel, Indiana UP, 1992, pp. 231–46.

Chrisman-Campbell, Kimberly. *The Way We Wed: A Global History of Wedding Fashion*. Running Press, 2020.

Chroniqueuse. *Photographs of Paris Life: A Record of the Politics, Art, Fashion and Anecdote of Paris During the Past Eighteen Months.* London, 1861.

Cohen, Philip N. "Nationalism and Suffrage: Gender Struggle in Nation-Building America." *Signs: Journal of Women in Culture and Society*, vol. 21, no. 3, 1996, pp. 707–27.

Colley, Linda. "Britishness and Otherness: An Argument." *Journal of British Studies*, vol. 31, no. 4, Oct. 1992, pp. 309–29.

———. *Britons: Forging the Nation 1707–1837.* Yale UP, 1992.

Craik, Jennifer. *Uniforms Exposed: From Conformity to Transgression.* Berg, 2005.

Crane, Diana. *Fashion and Its Social Agendas: Class, Gender, and Identity in Clothing.* U of Chicago P, 2000.

"Crinoline." Oxford English Dictionary, https://www.oed.com/dictionary/crinoline_n?tab=factsheet#7811460.

Cunnington, C. Willett. *English Women's Clothing in the Nineteenth Century.* 1937. Dover Publications, 1990.

Daly, Suzanne. "Kashmir Shawls in Mid-Victorian Novels." *Victorian Literature and Culture*, vol. 30, no. 1, 2002, pp. 237–56.

———. "Spinning Cotton: Domestic and Industrial Novels." *Victorian Studies*, vol. 50, no. 2, Winter 2008, pp. 272–78.

"The Dangers of Crinoline, Steel Hoops, &c." London, G. Vickers, ca. 1858.

David, Deirdre. *Rule Britannia: Women, Empire, and Victorian Writing.* Cornell UP, 1995.

Davies, Mel. "Corsets and Conception: Fashion and Demographic Trends in the Nineteenth Century." *Comparative Studies in Society and History*, vol. 24, no. 4, Oct. 1982, pp. 611–41.

Davis, Fred. *Fashion, Culture, and Identity.* U of Chicago P, 1992.

Dee, Phyllis Susan. "Female Sexuality and Triangular Desire in *Vanity Fair* and *The Mill on the Floss*." *Papers on Language and Literature*, vol. 35, no. 4, Fall 1999, pp. 391–416.

Dobson, Kit. "'An Insuperable Repugnance to Hearing Vice Called by Its Proper Name': Englishness, Gender and the Performed Identities of Rebecca and Amelia in Thackeray's *Vanity Fair*." *Victorian Review*, vol. 32, no. 2, 2006, pp. 1–25.

Douglas, Fanny (Mrs. Douglas). *The Gentlewoman's Book of Dress.* London, 1895.

Dress: A Few Words on Fashion and Her Idols. London, Saunders, Otley, and Co., 1859.

Dyer, Gary R. "The 'Vanity Fair' of Nineteenth-Century England: Commerce, Women, and the East in the Ladies' Bazaar." *Nineteenth-Century Literature*, vol. 46, no. 2, Sep. 1991, pp. 196–222.

Easthope, Antony. *Englishness and National Culture.* London: Routledge, 1999.

Eliot, George. *Middlemarch.* Edited by Gregory Maertz. Broadview Press, 2004.

———. "Silly Novels by Lady Novelists." 1856. https://commonreader.wustl.edu/c/silly-novels-by-lady-novelists/.

Ellis, Sarah Stickney. *The Women of England, Their Social Duties, and Domestic Habits*. London, 1839. *Internet Archive*, https://archive.org/details/womenofenglandth00ellirich/page/8/mode/2up.

———. *The Daughters of England, Their Position in Society, Character & Responsibilities*. New York, 1842. *WikiSource*, https://en.wikisource.org/wiki/The_Daughters_of_England.

Entwistle, Joanne. *The Fashioned Body: Fashion, Dress, and Modern Social Theory*. Polity Press, 2000.

Essig, Laurie. "'All the World Was There' and Other White Lies About the Royal Wedding." *QED: A Journal in GLBTQ Worldmaking*, vol. 3, no. 2, Summer 2016, pp. 35–55.

Farkas, Carol-Ann. "Beauty Is as Beauty Does: Action and Appearance in Brontë and Eliot. *Dickens Studies Annual*, vol. 29, 2000, pp. 323–49.

"Fashion History Timeline." Fashion Institute of Technology, https://fashionhistory.fitnyc.edu/1840-queen-victorias-wedding-dress/.

Fashion Museum Bath. "Jolly's of Bath," Batmc I.28.83/5/5b/5c.

Fenwick, Julie. "Mothers of Empire in Elizabeth Gaskell's *Cranford*." *English Studies in Canada*, vol. 23, no. 4, Dec. 1997, pp. 409–26.

Festa, Lynn. "Cosmetic Differences: The Changing Faces of England and France." *Studies in Eighteenth-Century Culture*, vol. 34, 2005, pp. 25–54.

Finnegan, Margaret Mary. *Selling Suffrage: Consumer Culture and Votes for Women*. Columbia UP, 1999.

Fisher, Judith Law. "Siren and Artist: Contradiction in Thackeray's Aesthetic Ideal." *Nineteenth-Century Fiction*, vol. 39, no. 4, Mar 1985, pp. 392–419.

Flanders, Judith. *Inside the Victorian Home: A Portrait of Domestic Life in Victorian England*. WW Norton and Company, 2004.

Flint, Kate. "The Materiality of *Middlemarch*." *Middlemarch in the 21st Century*, edited by Karen Chase, Oxford UP, 2006, pp. 104–41.

Foster, Helen Bradley, and Donald Clay Johnson. "Introduction." *Wedding Dress Across Cultures*, edited by Helen Bradley Foster and Donald Clay Johnson, Berg, 2003, pp. 1–4.

Fowler, Rowena. "Cranford: Cow in Grey Flannel or Lion Couchant?" *Studies in English Literature, 1500–1900*, vol. 24, no. 4, Autumn 1984, pp. 717–29.

Gaskell, Elizabeth. "The Cage at Cranford." *Cranford*, edited by Elizabeth Porges Watson. 1863. Oxford UP, 1998, pp. 169–79.

———. *Cranford*. Edited by Elizabeth Porges Watson, 1853. Oxford UP, 1998.

———. *North and South*. Edited by Patricia Ingham. 1855. Penguin Books, 1995.

Gilbert, David. "Urban Outfitting: The City and the Spaces of Fashion Culture." *Fashion Cultures: Theories, Explorations and Analysis*, edited by Stella Bruzzi and Pamela Church Gibson, Routledge, 2000, pp. 7–24.

Goodrum, Alison. "Land of Hip and Glory: Fashioning the 'Classic' National Body." *Dressed to Impress: Looking the Part*, edited by William J. F. Keenan, Berg, 2001, pp. 85–104.

Green, Barbara. "From Visible *Flaneuse* to Spectacular Suffragette? The Prison, the Street, and the Sites of Suffrage." *Discourse*, vol. 17, no. 2, Winter 1994-1995, pp. 67–97.

Hahn, Hazen. "Fashion Discourses in Fashion Magazines and Madame de Girardin's *Lettres parisiennes* in July-Monarchy France (1830–48)." *Fashion Theory*, vol. 9, no. 2, 2005, pp. 205–28.

Hammond, Mary. "Thackeray's Waterloo: History and War in *Vanity Fair*." *Literature and History*, vol. 11, no. 2, 2002, pp. 19–38.

Harvey, John. *Men in Black*. U of Chicago P, 1995.

Hasseler, Terri. "Mr. Punch's Crinoline Anxiety: The Indian Rebellion and the Rhetoric of Dress." *Comedy, Fantasy, and Colonialism*, edited by Graeme Harper, Continuum, 2002, pp. 117–39.

Haweis, Mary Eliza. *The Art of Beauty*. 1878. Rpt. in *The Art of Beauty and The Art of Dress*. Garland, 1978.

——. *The Art of Dress*. London, Chatto and Windus, 1879.

Heaton, Sarah. "Wayward Wedding Dresses: Fabricating Horror in Dressing Rituals of Femininity." *Fashioning Horror: Dressing to Kill on Screen and in Literature*, edited by Julia Petrov and Gudrun D Whitehead, Bloomsbury, 2017, pp. 83–99.

Helland, Janice. "'Caprices of Fashion': Handmade Lace in Ireland 1883-1907." *Textile History*, vol. 39, no. 2, Nov. 2008, pp. 193–222.

Hentschell, Roze. "Treasonous Textiles: Foreign Cloth and the Construction of Englishness." *Journal of Medieval and Early Modern Studies*, vol. 32, no. 3, Fall 2002, pp. 543–70.

Hoganson, Kristin. "The Fashionable World: Imagined Communities of Dress." *After the Imperial Turn: Thinking with and Through the Nation*, edited by Antoinette Burton, Duke UP, 2003, pp. 260–78.

Hollander, Anne. *Seeing Through Clothes*. U of California P, 1993.

——. *Sex and Suits*. Kodansha, 1995.

Holmes, Elizabeth. *HRH: So Many Thoughts on Royal Style*. Celadon Books, 2020.

Houston, Natalie M. "George Eliot's Material History: Clothing and Realist Narrative." *Studies in the Literary Imagination*, vol. 29, no. 1, Spring 1996, pp. 23–33.

Howlett, Caroline. "Femininity Slashed: Suffragette Militancy, Modernism and Gender." *Modernist Sexualities*, edited by Hugh Stevens and Caroline Howlett, Manchester UP, 2000, pp. 72–91.

Hughes, Clair. *Dressed in Fiction*. Bloomsbury, 2005.

Irwin, John. *The Kashmir Shawl* (Victoria and Albert Museum). Her Majesty's Stationery Office, 1973.

Jadwin, Lisa. "The Seductiveness of Female Duplicity in *Vanity Fair*." *SEL: Studies in English Literature*, vol. 32, no. 4, Autumn 1992, pp. 663–87.

Joannou, Maroula. " 'Chloe Liked Olivia': The Woman Scientist, Sex and Suffrage." *Literature, Science, Psychoanalysis, 1830–1970*, edited by Helen Small and Trudi Tate, Oxford UP, 2003, pp. 195–211.

Joslin, Katherine. *Edith Wharton and the Making of Fashion.* U of New Hampshire P, 2011.

Kaplan, Joel H., and Sheila Stowell. *Theatre and Fashion: Oscar Wilde to the Suffragettes*, Cambridge UP, 1994.

Keen, Suzanne. "Quaker Dress, Sexuality, and the Domestication of Reform in the Victorian Novel." *Victorian Literature and Culture*, vol. 30, no. 1, 2002, pp. 211–36.

Keenan, William J. F. "Dress Freedom: The Personal and the Political." *Dressed to Impress: Looking the Part*, edited by William J. F. Keenan, Berg, 2001, pp. 179–96.

Kociolek, Katarzyna. "London's Suffragettes, *Votes for Women*, and Fashion." *Anglica: An International Journal of English Studies*, vol. 27, no. 1, 2018, 81–95.

Kortsch, Christine Bayles. *Dress Culture in Late Victorian Women's Fiction: Literacy, Textiles, and Activism.* Routledge, 2009.

Lang, Cady. "Every Detail About Meghan Markle's Givenchy Royal Wedding Dress." May 19, 2018, https://time.com/5245809/meghan-markle-royal-wedding-dress/.

Langland, Elizabeth. "Inventing Reality: The Ideological Commitments of George Eliot's *Middlemarch*." *Narrative*, vol. 2, no. 2, May 1994, pp. 87–111.

———. "Nation and Nationality: Queen Victoria in the Developing Narrative of Englishness." *Telling Tales: Gender and Narrative Form in Victorian Literature and Culture*. Ohio State UP, 2002, pp. 111–29.

LeFavour, Cree. "Acting 'Natural': *Vanity Fair* and the Unmasking of Anglo-American Sentiment." *Sullen Fires Across the Atlantic: Essays in Transatlantic Romanticism*, edited by Lance Newman, Chris Koenig-Woodyard, and Joel Pace, 2006, https://romantic-circles.org/sites/default/files/2024-08/RC_Praxis_2006_Sullen%20Fires%20Across%20the%20Atlantic-Essays%20in%20Transatlantic%20Romanticism.pdf.

Legon, Edward. "Bound Up with Meaning: The Politics and Memory of Ribbon Wearing in Restoration England and Scotland." *Journal of British Studies*, vol. 56, Jan. 2017, pp. 27–50.

Linton, Eliza Lynn. "Nearing the Rapids." *Prose by Victorian Women: An Anthology*, edited by Andrea Broomfield and Sally Mitchell. 1868. Routledge, 1996, pp. 378–86.

Litvak, Joseph. *Strange Gourmets: Sophistication, Theory, and the Novel.* Duke UP, 1997.

Loeb, Lori Anne. *Consuming Angels: Advertising and Victorian Women*. Oxford UP, 1994.

London Museum. *"Description." Roxey Ann Caplin Corset*. Object ID: 37.161/137.161/1, https://www.londonmuseum.org.uk/collections/v/object-76190/corset/.

London Museum. *"Memento of Women's Coronation Procession to Demand Votes for Women Order of March and Descriptive Programme," 17 June 1911*. Suffragette Collection.

London Museum. "Photograph of Indian Suffragettes on the Women's Coronation Procession 17 June 1911." Accession no. 001489. Suffragette Collection.

London Museum. *Postcards*. Accession no. 50.82/1722. Suffragette Collection.

London Museum. *Prison Letters, Police Summons, Prison Records, "Leonora Tyson letter collection from Holloway," addressed "My Dearest Diana" on Sunday March 24, 1912 12:30 p.m.* Suffragette Collection.

London Museum. "Stockings." Accession no. 55.29a–b. Permanent Collection.

London Museum. "Thomson's Empress crinoline, red." Accession no. 46.33/12/LW.COS.U.P4.7.

London Museum. *Tyson, Leonora. Letter to Diana. 24 Mar. 1912.* Suffragette Collection.

London Museum. *"Women's Suffrage Calendar for 1899."* Accession no. 50.82/106. Suffragette Collection.

London Museum. *"A group of suffragettes in costume."* Accession no. 50.82/1307. Suffragette Collection.

Lupton, Christina. "Theorizing Surfaces and Depths: Gaskell's *Cranford*." *Criticism*, vol. 50, no. 2, Spring 2008, 235–54.

Lysack, Krista. *Come Buy, Come Buy: Shopping and the Culture of Consumption in Victorian Women's Writing*. Ohio UP, 2008.

———. "Goblin Markets: Victorian Women Shoppers at Liberty's Oriental Bazaar." *Nineteenth-Century Contexts*, vol. 27, no. 2, Jun. 2005, pp. 139–65.

MacDonald, Margaret F., Susan Grace Galassi, and Aileen Ribeiro. *Whistler, Women, and Fashion*. Yale UP, 2003.

Mahawatte, Royce. "The Sad Fortunes of 'Stylish Things': George Eliot and the Languages of Fashion." *Transglobal Fashion Narratives: Clothing Communication, Style Statements and Brand Storytelling*, edited by Anne Peirson-Smith and Joseph H. Hancock, II, Intellect, 2018, pp. 65–78.

Marcus, Sharon. *Between Women: Friendship, Desire, and Marriage in Victorian England*. Princeton UP, 2007.

———. "Reflections on Victorian Fashion Plates." *differences*, vol. 14, no. 3, Fall 2003, pp. 4–33.

Marks, Patricia. "'*Mon Pauvre Prisonnier*': Becky Sharp and the Triumph of Napoleon." *Studies in the Novel*, vol. 28, no. 1, Spring 1996, pp. 76–92.

Martineau, Harriet. "A Real Social Evil." *The Daily News*, October 15, 1861.

McClintock, Anne. *Imperial Leather: Race, Gender, and Sexuality in the Colonial Conquest.* Routledge, 1995.

McDowell, Colin. *Hats: Status, Style, and Glamour.* Rizzoli International Publications, 1992.

Meredith, George. *Diana of the Crossways.* 1897. Wildside Press, 2002.

Meyer, Susan. *Imperialism at Home: Race and Victorian Women's Fiction.* Cornell UP, 1996.

Meyer, Tamar. "Gender Ironies of Nationalism: Setting the Stage." *Gender Ironies of Nationalism: Sexing the Nation,* edited by Tamar Meyer, Routledge, 2000, pp. 1–22.

Mida, Ingrid E., and Alexandra Kim. *The Dress Detective: A Practical Guide to Object-Based Research in Fashion.* Bloomsbury, 2015.

Miller, Andrew H. *Novels Behind Glass: Commodity Culture and the Victorian Narrative.* Cambridge UP, 1995.

Moers, Ellen. *Literary Women: The Great Writers.* Oxford UP, 1977.

Moore, Sarah J. "Making a Spectacle of Suffrage: The National Woman Suffrage Pageant, 1913." *Journal of American Culture,* vol. 20, no. 1, Spring 1997, pp. 89–103.

Morgan, Marjorie. *National Identities and Travel in Victorian Britain.* Palgrave, 2001.

National Portrait Gallery. "This Portrait." George Eliot, https://www.npg.org.uk/collections/search/portrait/mw189744/George-Eliot.

Nita. "The World We Live In: On Frocks and Other Things." *Votes for Women,* November 5, 1909: 87.

———. "The World We Live In: Practical Notes on Present Fashions." *Votes for Women,* Apr. 29, 1910: 497.

O'Farrell, Mary Ann. *Telling Complexions: The Nineteenth-Century English Novel and the Blush.* Duke UP, 1997.

Oliphant, Margaret. *Phoebe Junior, A Last Chronicle of Carlingford.* Edited by Elizabeth Langland. 1876. Broadview Press, 2002.

Parkins, Wendy. "What to Wear to a Protest March: Identity Politics and Fashion in the Suffrage Movement." *Southern Review,* vol. 28, no. 1, Mar. 1995, pp. 69–82.

———. " 'The Epidemic of Purple, White and Green': Fashion and the Suffragette Movement in Britain 1908–1914." *Fashioning the Body Politic: Dress, Gender, Citizenship,* edited by Wendy Parkins, Berg, 2002, pp. 97–124.

Parrinder, Patrick. *Nation and Novel: The English Novel from Its Origins to the Present Day.* Oxford UP, 2006.

Patmore, Coventry. "The Angel in the House." 1854. Project Gutenberg, https://www.gutenberg.org/files/4099/4099-h/4099-h.htm.

Penner, Barbara. " 'A Vision of Love and Luxury': The Commercialization of Nineteenth-Century American Weddings." *Winterthur Portfolio,* vol. 39, no. 1, Spring 2004, pp. 1–20.

Pethick Lawrence, Emmeline. "The Purple, White, & Green." *The Women's Exhibition 1909, Programme.* London, Women's Social and Political Union, 1909, 13–14.

Picken, Mary Brooks. *A Dictionary of Costume and Fashion, Historic and Modern.* Dover Publications, 1999. Rpt. of *The Fashion Dictionary.* 1957.

Poon, Angelia. "Comic Acts of (Be)Longing: Performing Englishness in *Wonderful Adventures of Mrs. Seacole in Many Lands.*" *Victorian Literature and Culture,* vol. 35, no. 2, 2007, pp. 501–16.

Porter, Bernard. *The Absent-Minded Imperialists: Empire, Society, and Culture in Britain.* Oxford UP, 2004.

"Queen Victoria's Wedding Dress." Royal Collection Trust, https://www.rct.uk/collection/themes/trails/royal-weddings/queen-victorias-wedding-dress.

Rappaport, Erika Diane. *Shopping for Pleasure: Women in the Making of London's West End.* Princeton UP, 2000.

Robson, Jennifer. *The Gown: A Novel of the Royal Wedding.* William Morris, 2018.

Rolley, Katrina. "Fashion, Femininity and the Fight for the Vote." *Art History,* vol. 13, no. 1, Mar. 1990, pp. 47–71.

Rosenman, Ellen Bayuk. "Fear of Fashion; Or, How the Coquette Got Her Bad Name." *ANQ,* vol. 15, no. 3, Summer 2002, pp. 12–21.

Schmitt, Cannon. *Alien Nation: Nineteenth-Century Gothic Fictions and English Nationality.* U of Pennsylvania P, 1997.

Schor, Hilary. *Scheherazade in the Marketplace: Elizabeth Gaskell and the Victorian Novel.* Oxford UP, 1992.

Shannon, Brent. *The Cut of His Coat: Men, Dress, and Consumer Culture in Britain, 1860–1914.* Ohio UP, 2006.

Sharp, Joanne. "Gendering Nationhood: A Feminist Engagement with National Identity." *BodySpace: Destabilizing Geographies of Gender and Sexuality,* edited by Nancy Duncan, Routledge, 1996, pp. 97–108.

Sheets, Robin Ann. "Art and Artistry in *Vanity Fair.*" *ELH,* vol. 42, no. 3, Fall 1975, pp. 420–32.

"Shops That Suffered." *Votes for Women,* March 8, 1912, p. 353.

Shuttleworth, Sally. "Sexuality and Knowledge in *Middlemarch.*" *Nineteenth-Century Contexts,* vol. 19, 1996, pp. 425–41.

Simmel, Georg. "Fashion." *American Journal of Sociology,* vol. 62, no. 6, May 1957, pp. 541–58.

Simpson, Anne B. "Architects of the Erotic: H. G. Wells's 'New Women.'" *Seeing Double: Revisioning Edwardian and Modernist Literature,* edited by Carola M. Kaplan and Anne B. Simpson. St. Martin's Press, 1996, pp. 39–55.

"Some Press Descriptions." *Votes for Women,* March 8, 1912, p. 352.

"Some W.S.P.U. Shops." *Votes for Women,* October 6, 1911, p. 7.

Staniland, Kay, and Santina M. Levey. "Queen Victoria's Wedding Dress and Lace." *Costume,* vol. 17, no. 1, 1983, pp. 1–32.

Steele, Valerie. *Fashion and Eroticism: Ideals of Feminine Beauty from the Victorian Era to the Jazz Age.* Oxford UP, 1985.

———. *The Corset: A Cultural History.* Yale UP, 2004.

Summers, Leigh. *Bound to Please: A History of the Victorian Corset.* Berg, 2001.

Thackeray, William Makepeace. *Vanity Fair.* Edited by J. I. M. Stewart. 1848. Penguin Books, 1985.

Tickner, Lisa. *The Spectacle of Women: Imagery of the Suffrage Campaign 1907–1914.* The U of Chicago P, 1988.

Wahl, Kimberly. "Purity and Parity: The White Dress of the Suffrage Movement in Early Twentieth-Century Britain." *Colors in Fashion,* edited by Jonathan Faiers and Mary Westerman Bulgarella. Bloomsbury, 2016, pp. 21–33.

Wardrop, Daneen. *Emily Dickinson and the Labor of Clothing.* U of New Hampshire P, 2009.

Wells, H. G. *Ann Veronica.* Edited by Sita Schutt. 1909. Penguin Books, 2005.

Wessell, Adele. "Having Our Cake and Eating It Too: A Reading of Royal Wedding Cakes." *Australasian Journal of Popular Culture,* vol. 2, no. 1, 2013, pp. 47–56.

Whiteleys Spring Show of Fashion. Advertisement. *Votes for Women,* March 15, 1912, p. 380.

Wilson, Elizabeth. *Adorned in Dreams: Fashion and Modernity.* Rutgers UP, 2003.

Women's Library, London School of Economics. Brown, Myra Sadd. *Letter to Ernie. 20 March 1912. Militant Suffragettes, Index 1911–1912, No. 190, Box #6.1, 9/20/105, Box 4 vol. 10–22,* Autograph Letter Collection.

Women's Library, London School of Economics. *"Hugh Franklin and Elsie Duval Papers" Collection, Folder 3: Miscellaneous Paper.* Reference no. 7HFD/A/3, Box #FL226, 1908–1913.

Women's Library, London School of Economics. Marion, Kitty. *Autobiography. Unpublished ms.* Reference no. 7/KMA or 7/YYY6, Box FL639.

Women's Library, London School of Economics. *Militant Suffragettes, Index 1911–1912, No. 190, Box #6.1, 9/20/105, Box 4 vol. 10–22.* Autograph Letter Collection.

Women's Social and Political Union. *Memento of Women's Coronation Procession to Demand Votes for Women Order of March and Descriptive Programme,* London: The Woman's Press, 1911.

Wood, Ellen. *East Lynne.* Edited by Andrew Maunder. 1861. Broadview Press, 2000.

Woolf, Virginia. "George Eliot." *The Times Literary Supplement,* November 20, 1919, https://digital.library.upenn.edu/women/woolf/VW-Eliot.html.

Zlotnick, Susan. "Domesticating Imperialism: Curry and Cookbooks in Victorian England." *Frontiers,* vol. 16, no. 2–3, 1996, pp. 51–68.

Index

Page numbers in *italics* refer to figures.

advertising, 17, 120n21
Albert (Prince consort), 108
Allen, Emily, 108
Alter, Peter, 7
Anderson, Benedict, 13
"Angel in the House, The" (Patmore),
    14–15
Ann Veronica (Wells), 21, 86, 95–101,
    133n26; Ann Veronica, 95–101;
    Capes, 98–99, 100; Miss Miniver,
    95–96; Miss Stanley (aunt), 101;
    Mr. Stanley, 100; Stanley family, 100
Arch, Nigel, 109
aristocracy, 13, 50, 56, 125
Arnold, Jean, 66
Art of Beauty, The (Haweis), 52–53,
    59, 63
artificiality, 3, 4, 48–54, 57–62, 64, 77
Atkinson, Diane, 87
Audax, Frederick, 58–59

Barthes, Roland, 12
Batchelor, Jennie, 12
Bettans, Mary, 109
Between Women (Marcus), 15
Bidney, Jane, 109
blushing, 62
Bohleke, Karin J., 17

Bowlby, Rachel, 17
Breward, Christopher, 17
British Empire, 7, 18, 20, 28, 29,
    30, 36, 94, 108; Commonwealth
    countries, 111
Britishness. *See* Englishness
Britons: Forging the Nation 1707–1837
    (Colley), 7
brocade, 125n9
Brontë, Charlotte, 127n5
Brontë sisters, 65
Brown, Myra Sadd, 88
Buck, Anne M., 15
Bull, John, 118n9, 122n13
Bull, Mrs. John, 118n9
Burslem, Lillian, *83*, 84
Burton, Sarah, 112, 113
bustles, 123n1

"Cage at Cranford" (Gaskell), 42–43,
    44; Amazons, 44–45; Fanny, 42;
    Mary Smith, 42–44; Miss Arly, 42;
    Miss Pole, 42–43; Mr. Hoggins, 43;
    Mrs. Gordon, 42
calashes, 43, 123n18
calico, 122n16
Camilla (Queen), 112
Caplin, Roxey Ann, 47, 48, 123–124n2

148 | Index

Carried Away (Bowlby), 17
Cass, Jeffrey, 30
Cavallaro, Dani, 13
Chalus, Elaine, 11
Charles I (King), 128n14
Charles II (Prince; now King), 112
Chrisman-Campbell, Kimberly, 111, 112
Chroniqueuse, 2, 3–4, 52, 53
class status, 14
clogs, 21, *97, 98*
Colley, Linda, 7, 16
colonialism, 134n2
colonization, 36
corsets: concerns about, 19, 63–64, 119, 123n1, 126n15; construction of, 48, 57; decline of, 8, 115; in literature, 58, 124n3, 126n13; poorly fitting, 58; Roxey Ann Caplin's, *47,* 48, 84, 123–124n2; wearing of, 13, 115
cosmetics, 16, 120n19
COVID-19 pandemic, 105, 113
Crane, Diana, 6, 12, 28
Cranford (Gaskell), 17–19, 20, 24–27, 29–33, 35, 37, 39–45, 68, 72, 79; Amazons, 17, 19, 30–33, 40, 42, 72, 121; Captain Brown, 30; Mary Smith, 31, 32–33, 35, 41–42; Miss Matty, 33, 35, 39–42; Mrs. Jenkyns, 39–40; Peter, 33, 35, 37, 39–40; Signor Brunoni, 41
crinolines: dangers of, 24, 70–72, 115, 120–121n1, 123n1, 128n9; definition of, 24; French origin of, 18, 24–25, 43, 44, 70; in literature, 20, 24–25, 27, 42, 43; popularity of, 8, 14, 24, 115, 122n15; red, *23, 24,* 25, 48, 84; worn by Eliot, 68
Cullwick, Hannah, 15
Cunnington, C. Willett, 12, 41–42

Daly, Suzanne, 34, 37
Daniel Deronda (Eliot), 65, 66
Davis, Fred, 5, 12–13
Diana (Princess), 112, 113–114
Diana of the Crossways (Meredith), 19, 126n12
Dobson, Kit, 51
dolls, 15, 54
domestic space, 16; Englishwomen presiding over, 44–45; gendered, 25–26
Douglas, Fanny, 16, 34, 44
dress: democracy of, 28; details of, 6, 8, 20; disregard for, 28; economy of, 72; Englishness of, 40–45; vs. fashion, 19; ignorance of, 49; national, 28; Quaker, 127n7, 130n24; as reflection of inner mind, 27–28; used for communication, 15; women's obsession with, 8. *See also* dressing; fashion; foreign dress
dress codes, 14
Dress Culture in Late Victorian Women's Fiction (Kortsch), 13
Dress Detective, The, 19
dress reform movement, 48
dress styles: empire waist gowns, 14; tighter skirts, 14; wider skirts, 14
Dressed in Fiction (Hughes), 5, 75
dresses, 55, 56–57, 76; worn by Ann Veronica, 100–101; worn by George Eliot, 68–69. *See also* wedding dresses
dressing: improper, 19; meaning of, 2; for the nation, 22; for other women, 14, 15, 54, 57, 73, 76, 120n7; public vs. private, 5; for seduction, 15. *See also* dress; fashion

East Lynne (Wood), 11
Easthope, Antony, 16

Edith Wharton and the Making of Fashion (Joslin), 5

Eliot, George, 21, 127n5, 127n6; *Daniel Deronda*, 65, 66; *Middlemarch*, 21, 65–81, 127n4, 128n11, 130n27; photograph, 67–69, *67, 68*; *Romola*, 65, 66, 127n3

Elizabeth Bennett, 15

Elizabeth II (Queen), 109, 110–111, 112, 135n8

Ellis, Sarah Stickney, 20, 26, 27–28, 29, 33, 59, 93

Emily Dickinson and the Labor of Clothing (Wardrop), 5

English Burberry check, 119n11

English Women's Clothing in the Nineteenth Century (Cunnington), 12, 41–42

Englishness, 7–8, 16, 26, 27; changing definition of, 45; in Cranford, 37; of dress, 40–45; of the good Englishwoman, 27–40

Englishness and National Culture (Easthope), 16

Eugenie (Princess), 22, 107, 109, 112–113, 135n9

Evans, Mary Ann. *See* Eliot, George

fabrics. *See* textiles

fashion: American, 17; awareness of, 78; bottom-up model, 120n16; changes in, 5–6; choices contrary to, 32–33, 74–75, 80, 129n19, 129n20; communication by means of, 13; and concealed weapons, 134n30; consumption and reading of, 54–55; in Cranford, 32–33; as cultural object, 12; vs. dress, 19; and eroticism, 15; excessive attention to, 21; and the female

body, 63–64; as feminine weakness, 4; French, 11–12, 17, 20, 24, 27, 40–41, 42–44, 45, 52, 70, 79, 119n13, 120n20, 122n14, 123n20, 126n12; function of, 2–3; global system of, 12; importance of, 3–4, 14; indicating wealth and status, 5, 12–13, 14, 27, 28, 33–34, 37, 39, 119–120n15; interpretation of, 5–6, 12–13, 32–33; in Ireland, 89, 92, *92*, 93; local production of, 9–18; in London, 11–12; love of, 21; manipulation of, 6; men's vs. women's, 99; and national identity, 41, 51–52, 58, 64, 86; and nationalism, 4–9, 11, 13, 19, 89–94, *90, 92*, 111, 114–115, 121n4, 132n18; nationality of, 4; natural vs. artificial style, 50–53; outward displays of, 8; as outward marker of inner self, 28; and patriotism, 11; personal alterations, 123n21; and politics, 11; in Scotland, 21, 34–35, 84, 87, 89–90, 91, 92, *92*, 93, 121n8; and sex appeal, 15, 120n18; significance of, 11, 13–14; as signifier of gender and sexuality, 12, 14; as tool, 9; used to convey character, 6; Victorian, 52–53; in Wales, 87, 89, 92, *92*, 133n22; and the women's suffrage movement, 84–94, 102, 130n4, 134n31. *See also* dress; dressing

Fashion, Culture, and Identity (Davis), 12–13

Fashion and Eroticism (Steele), 15, 41, 52

Fashion and Its Social Agendas (Crane), 12

Fashion History Timeline, 110

fashion industry, 17

Fashion Museum (Bath), 105–106
Fashion System, The (Barthes), 12
Fashioning the Frame (Cavallaro & Warwick), 13
female gaze, 54, 55
feminine power, 4, 70, 94
femininity, 15, 104; and dress, 129n21; of George Eliot, 69; English, 51; marketing, 54; middle-class, 133n25; and the women's suffrage movement, 21, 85, 88, 89
feminism, 133n27; activists, 84; in *Ann Veronica*, 99; and fashion, 85–86; and politics, 95; and the women's suffrage movement, 103
feminists: negative portrayals of, 95. *See also* suffragettes; suffragists
Finnegan, Margaret Mary, 94
FITNYC (Fashion Institute of Technology in New York City), 110
Flanders, Judith, 14
flappers, 120n18
Flint, Kate, 66
flounces, 52
foreign dress: crinolines, 27; Indian shawl, 8; Kashmir shawls, 10, 27, 29, 35–39; turbans (women's), 8, 27
Foster, Helen Bradley, 110
Fowler, Rowena, 33
France, and the fashion industry, 110. *See also* Paris

Gaskell, Elizabeth, 24, 26, 29, 65, 66, 81, 122n11; "The Cage at Cranford," 42–43, 44; *Cranford*, 17–19, 20, 24–27, 29–33, 35, 37, 39–45, 68, 72, 79; *Mary Barton*, 19, 29, 128n10; *North and South*, 27, 37–39; *Ruth*, 29, 128n10
gender, performative, 125n7
gender hierarchy, 134n2
gender roles, 21

Gentlewoman's Book of Dress (Douglas), 16, 44
Gilbert, David, 11
Gown, The: A Novel of the Royal Wedding (Robson), 111
Grace (Princess), 112
Green, Barbara, 84

hairstyles, 74–75, 96–97, 99–100
Hall, Agusta (Lady Llanover), 133n22
handkerchiefs, 11
Harlaxton College, 113
Harry (Prince), 20, 112
Hartnell, Normal, 111
Hasseler, Terri, 24
Haweis, Mary Eliza, 52–53, 59, 60, 63
Hentschell, Roze, 10
heteroeroticism, 54
Hint from Modesty to the Ladies of England, A (Audax), 58–59
Hollander, Anne, 3, 6, 8
Holmes, Elizabeth, 111, 112
home, symbolic space of, 25–26, 121n2
home industries, 34
hoops, 70
Hope, Mrs. Thomas Radford, 106–107
HRH: So Many Thoughts on Royal Style (Holmes), 111
Hughes, Clair, 5, 66, 75

identity: as English citizen, 7; national, 92–93, 118n7, 119n11, 126n13, 132n18; social construction of, 6
imperialism, 29, 118–119n10, 121n5
innocence, 29, 30, 49, 51, 61, 62, 98
Inside the Victorian Home (Flanders), 14
International Woman Suffrage Alliance, 131n10

Jane Eyre, 15, 127n7
jewelry, 55, 73–74, 76, 128n14,
    128–129n15, 129nn17–18
Johnson, Donald Clay, 110
Johnson, Fleur, 106
Jolly's Department Store, 106
Jones, Owen, 130n27
Joslin, Katherine, 5

Kaplan, Joel H., 86
Keenan, William J. F., 11, 85
Kenney, Annie, 133n25
Kensington Palace, 113–114
Kortsch, Christine Bayles, 13

lace: Carrickmacross, 112–113; collar,
    68; Honiton, 107, 109, 110, 111,
    134n6, 134–135n7; repurposed,
    125n9
Langland, Elizabeth, 108
Lawrence, Pethick, 91
Linton, Eliza Lynn, 16, 20, 93
Literary Women (Moers), 69
Litvak, Joseph, 57
Llanover, Lady (Augusta Hall),
    133n22
Loeb, Lori Ann, 16
Lysack, Krista, 69

Marcus, Sharon, 12, 15, 17, 41, 54,
    55, 75
Margaret (Princess), 112
Marion, Kitty, 103
Markle, Meghan, 20, 22, 107, 109,
    112–113, 114
Marks, Patricia, 55
Marschner, Joanne, 109
Martineau, Harriet, 70–72, 75, 76, 81
Mary (Queen), 112
Mary Barton (Gaskell), 19, 29, 128n10
masculinity: English, 29, 37; in
    Victorian England, 7–8

material culture, 5, 19, 66, 130n22
McQueen, Alexander, 112, 113, 135n10
Melbourne (Lord), 110
men's clothing, 124n3, 129n21, 130n26
Meredith, George, 126n12
Meyer, Tamar, 11, 29
Michels, Louis, 16
middle class, 14, 17, 26, 33, 34, 49,
    56, 85, 121n5, 133n25
Middlemarch (Eliot), 21, 65–81,
    127n4, 128n11, 130n27; Casaubon,
    76; Celia Brooke, 72, 73–74, 76,
    77; Dorothea Brooke, 21, 66, 67,
    69–70, 72–80, 127n4, 127nn7–8,
    128nn12–13, 129nn19–20, 130n22;
    Gwendolyn, 69; Harriet Bulstrode,
    80; Lydgate, 77, 80, 130n26; Mr.
    Bulstrode, 80; Rosamond Vincy, 66,
    67, 69–70, 77–80, 127n4, 130n25;
    Will Ladislaw, 76, 80
Middleton, Kate, 22, 107, 109,
    112–113, 114, 135n10
Miller, Andrew H., 66, 66–67
milliners, 122n14
modernization, 31, 40
Moers, Ellen, 69

National Union of Women's Suffrage
    Societies (NUWSS), 86. *See also*
    suffragists
nationalism, 27, *90*, 132n17; and the
    crinoline, 24; and fashion, 4–9, 11,
    13, 19, 89–94, *90*, *92*, 111, 114–115,
    121n4, 132n18; and gender, 118–
    119n10; ideology of, 16; and local
    products, 9–18; women's, 16–17
Nita, 85, 89, 93
North and South (Gaskell), 27, 37–39;
    Aunt Shaw, 37–38; Edith, 37–38,
    39; Helen, 37; Henry Lennox,
    38–39; Margaret, 37–39; Mrs.
    Gibson, 37

Novels Behind Glass (Miller), 66–67

O'Farrell, Mary Ann, 62
Oliphant, Margaret, 3

Pankhurst, Emmeline, 87, 88, 131n7
Paris, 40, 44, 52, 60, 89
Patmore, Coventry, 14–15
patriotism, 11, 19, 26, 28
performative activism, 84, 95
petticoats, 20, 52, 122n15
Philip Mountbatten, 111
Phoebe Junior (Oliphant), 2, 3, 6
Pilotto, Peter, 135n9
Poon, Angelia, 7

racial hierarchy, 134n2
racism, 132n17
Rappaport, Erika, 102
ribbons, 11, 128n11
Robson, Jennifer, 111
Rolley, Katrina, 86, 87
Romola (Eliot), 65, 66, 127n3
Rosenman, Ellen Bayuk, 54
Royal Collection Trust, 109–110
Royal School of Needlework, 113
Royal Wedding Dresses (Arch & Marschner), 109
Ruth (Gaskell), 29, 128n10

Salisbury, Marquess of, 134–135n7
satin, 110, 111, 125–126n11, 135n8
Schmitt, Cannon, 30
Schor, Hilary M., 40
Scottish kilts, 21, *92*, 93
Seeing Through Clothes (Hollander), 3
Selling Suffrage (Finnegan), 94
Seneca Falls convention, 94
Sharp, Joanne, 8
shawls, 21, 55, *97*, 98; Indian, 8, 10, 122n11; Irish, *92*; Kashmir (Cashmir), 8, 27, 29, 35–39, 121n9, 122nn10–12, 125–126n11

Sheets, Robin Ann, 50–51, 55
silk, 109, 111, 134n1, 135n8
slavery, 134n2
slips, 125–126n11
Steele, Valerie, 15, 41, 52
Stevenson, Robert Louis, 117n4
stockings, 83–84, *83*
stovepipe hat, *92*, 93
Stowell, Sheila, 86
suffragettes: American, 94, 131n9; British, 87, 91, 92–94, *92*, *97*, 98, 101, 131n9; in the British Empire, *90*, *92*, 94; Lilian Burslem, *83*, 84; clothing worn by, 21, *83*, 84, 85–94, 98, 102, 103–104; colors worn by, 84, 85; fictional, 94–101; from India, *90*, 91; Irish, 91, 92–93, *92*; Kitty Marion, 103; militant, 89, 94, 96, 96–97, *97*, *97*, 101, 101–104, 102, 134n31; negative portrayals of, 131n7; Emmeline Pankhurst, 87, 88, 131n7; performative activism of, 84, 95; in prison, 87–88, 96–99; radical, 95–96; Scottish, 91, 92–93, *92*; vs. suffragists (use of term), 131n5; Leonora Tyson, 87–88; wearing national dress, 87, 89–92, *90*, *92*, 93; Welsh, 91, 92–93, *92*. *See also* Women's Social and Political Union (WSPU); women's suffrage movement
suffragists: American, 94; British, 94; clothing worn by, 86–87, 89–90, 93–94, 103–104, 118n9; negative portrayals of, 85, 95, 101; stereotypes of, 85; vs. suffragettes (use of term), 131n5. *See also* National Union of Women's Suffrage Societies (NUWSS)

textiles: brocade, 125n9; cotton, 122n16; English, 109–110; English Burberry check, 119n11; domestic,

34–35; and fashion, 19, 20; foreign, 34–35, 121n7; Indian, 34, 122n16; satin, 110, 111, 125–126n11, 135n8; significance of, 34; silk, 109, 111, 134n1, 135n8; woolen industry, 134–135n7. *See also* lace
Thackeray, William, 6, 20–21, 31, 66; *Vanity Fair*, 20–21, 31, 47–64
Thewlis, Dora, 133n23
tiaras, 112. *See also* jewelry
Tickner, Lisa, 87, 94
trains, 123n1
turbans (women's), 8, 20, 27, 41–42; Arab, 42; Italian, 42
Tyson, Leonora, 87–88

umbrellas, 20, 33
Union Jack, *92*, 93, 95

vanity, 5, 24, 40, 71, 73–74, 76, 79, 80–81, 103, 128n10, 128n15
Vanity Fair (Thackeray), 19, 20–21, 31, 47–64; Amelia Sedley Osborne, 20–21, 48–51, 56–64, 77, 125n7, 125nn9–10, 125–126n11, 126n14; Becky (Rebecca) Sharp Crawley, 21, 48–51, 53–64, 75, 124n5, 124–126n6, 125nn7–11, 126n14, 126n16; Dobbin, 48, 62; George Osborne, 48–49, 57, 58, 61, 63; Jos Sedley, 62; Lord Steyne, 55–56; Miss Crawley, 59–60; Miss Pinkerton, 61; Miss Swartz, 19; Mrs. O'Dowd, 61; Rawdon Crawley, 50, 55, 60
Victoria (Queen), 7, 11, 21, 22, 29, 38, 71, 106, 107–110, 111, 114, 134nn2–4, 134n6, 134–135n7
Votes for Women, 85, 89, 93, 102, 103, 130n4

Wardrop, Daneen, 5
Warwick, Alexandra, 13

wedding cakes, 108
Wedding Dress Across Cultures, 110
wedding dresses, 21–22; at the Bath Fashion Museum, 106; Princess Diana, 113–114; Elizabeth II (Queen), 110–111, 135n8; Mrs. Thomas Radford Hope, 106–107; Princess Eugenie, 22, 135n10; Princess Grace, 112; Meghan Markle, 22, 112–113; Kate Middleton, 22, 112–113, 135n10; Victoria (Queen), 21–22, 106, 107–110, 134n4, 134n6, 134–135n7
Wells, H. G., 133n27; *Ann Veronica*, 21, 86, 95–101, 133n26
William (Prince), 112
Wilson, Elizabeth, 5
Wives and Daughters (Gaskell), 29
women: agency of, 9, 18, 70–71, 74–75, 115; of color, 19, 20, 132n15; English, 26, 58–59, 60, 64, 70–71, 79, 86, 89, 92–93, *92*, 103; foreign, 20; French, 16–17, 20, 49, 51, 52–53, 57, 60, 64, 89, 124n5, 125n8; and genre fiction, 66; from India, *90*, 91; Irish, 92–93, *92*; literacy of, 13; as objects/ornaments, 77, 79; and politics, 85; pregnant, 58, 100, 126n14, 126n15; as "queens of society," 16; roles of, 21, 27; Scottish, 92–93, *92*; separate spheres of, 2, 117n1; as symbol of nationalism, 8, 20, 29, 44–45; Welsh, 92–93, *92*, 132–133n20; working-class, 19. *See also* suffragettes; suffragists
Women of England, The (Ellis), 26, 59
Women's Coronation Procession, 89–93, *90*, *92*
Women's Exhibition (1909), 91
women's magazines, 3, 117n3
women's rights movement, 8, 94

Women's Social and Political Union (WSPU), 83–87, 95, 97, 101, 130n3, 131n7, 133n25; attack on the West End, 101–104. *See also* suffragettes
women's suffrage movement, 20, 21, 81, 83–104, 133n27; attack on the West End, 101–104; and fashion, 84–94, 130n4, 134n31; international, 131n10. *See also* suffragettes; suffragists
Wood, Ellen, 11
Woolf, Virginia, 65
Worth, Charles Frederick, 17